A NARRATIVE OF THE
LIFE OF MRS. MARY JEMISON

A Narrative of the
Life of Mrs. Mary Jemison

By James E. Seaver

With an Introduction by June Namias

University of Oklahoma Press : Norman and London

E
83
.J46
S42
1992

By June Namias

First Generation: In the Words of Twentieth-Century Immigrants, rev.
ed. (Boston, 1978)
A Narrative of the Life of Mrs. Mary Jemison, by James E. Seaver
(ed.) (Norman, 1992)

Library of Congress Cataloging-in-Publication Data

Seaver, James E. (James Everett), 1787–1827.
    A narrative of the life of Mrs. Mary Jemison / James E.
Seaver ; [edited and] with an introduction by June Namias.—1st
ed.
        p.   cm.
    Reprint. Originally published: Canandaigua, N.Y. : J. D.
Bemis, 1824.
    Includes bibliographical references (p.   ) and index.
    ISBN 0-8061-2381-8
    1. Jemison, Mary, 1743–1833. 2. Seneca Indians—Captivities.
3. Pioneers—Genesee River Valley (Pa. and N.Y.)—Biography.
4. Genesee River Valley (Pa. and N.Y.)—Biography. I. Namias,
June. II. Title.
[E83.J46S42   1992]
974.7'004975—dc20
[B]   91-50871
                                                               CIP

Published by the University of Oklahoma Press, Norman, Publishing
Division of the University. Copyright © 1992 by June Namias. All
rights reserved. Manufactured in the U.S.A. First edition.

CONTENTS

v

ILLUSTRATIONS

MAPS

EDITOR'S ACKNOWLEDGMENTS

THIS new edition has its origins in my first reading of *A Narrative of the Life of Mrs. Mary Jemison* as part of a first-year doctoral study on captivity narratives. During that reading I was struck by the significance of Jemison's life. Here was a woman who lived nearly a century, through great transformations, marriage to two husbands, the births of eight children, and in three cultures: colonial frontier Pennsylvania, mid- to late-eighteenth-century Seneca, and the early industrial American republic. As I continued my work, Jemison remained on my mind. I wanted her life to reach a broader audience.

Many institutions have helped support this effort. During my years of graduate study in the History of American Civilization program at Brandeis University my work was supported by the Irving and Rose Crown Fellowship. Jemison was also on my mind during my residencies at the Millay Colony for the Arts and for two summer months in Mohawk country at the Blue Mountain Center in Blue Mountain, New York. A Smithsonian Fellowship introduced me to Rayna Green of the American Indian Program at the National Museum of American History. Rayna helped open to me the world of the fine Smithsonian libraries and museums and gave me the chance to meet Indian people, learn Seneca dances, and talk with other scholars at the Smithsonian. Support from the History of the Book in American Culture seminar at the American Antiquarian Society in Worcester, Massachusetts, introduced me to the art of studying multiple editions. Chica-

ix

go's Newberry Library generously offered me a fellowship to use their outstanding collections. Finally, the history faculty and the Kelly Fund of the Massachusetts Institute of Technology provided generous financial and moral support for this latest reincarnation of the Jemison saga.

There are many people without whom this book would not have happened. My first words about Mary Jemison were written for John Demos. He has probably seen more of Jemison than he might have liked, but his keen mind and continuing encouragement cheered me on. Joyce Antler and Donald Worster also contributed their thoughts to writing I have done on Jemison. Julie Roy Jeffrey suggested I work on a new edition; her suggestions and ongoing support have been sincerely appreciated. The work of G. Peter Jemison got me thinking about a Jemison edition with an appropriate Seneca cover. Tom Willcockson of the Hermon Dunlap Smith Center for the History of Cartography at the Newberry Library provided an excellent set of maps. Tom Cook, historian for Letchworth State Park, took me for a tour of the Jemison lands and shared with me both his view of Iroquois life and his knowledge of the archives in central New York. I owe special thanks to Rayna Green, Carol F. Karlsen, Wendy Gamber, Daniel A. Cohen, William N. Fenton, Tom Cook, Arthur Kaledin, Daria Donnelly, Elise Marienstas, Mimi Grosser, Neal Salisbury, and Robert Slavin, who read and commented on earlier drafts of the Introduction to this edition or on my other writing on Jemison. Through the Undergraduate Research Opportunities Program at the Massachusetts Institute of Technology, Seth Gordon helped with suggestions for the map and the manuscript, and Tona Hangen assisted with bibliographic citations. Natasha Anisimov, Carol Zemel, Susan Armitage, Lissa Gifford, and Carla Borden helped in a variety of ways.

By giving me full reign over the "little house" in Vermont, Mimi Grosser became somewhat my, and hence Jemison's, patron. It was there that I first read two Seaver editions, and saw my first blue heron—a sure Seneca sign that I would continue my work to the end. Charlotte Cecil Raymond, my literary agent and great friend, has monitored this project a long time and deserves some credit for its final publication.

I am especially grateful to those librarians, curators, museums, and libraries that facilitated my work in the quest for Mary Jemison: James P. Roan, at the National Museum of American History; the staff of the Goldfarb Library, Brandeis University; the staff of the American Antiquarian Society; Kathleen Green at the Dewey Library of the Massachusetts Institute of Technology; Karl Kabelac of the Department of Rare Books and Special Collections, Rush Rheese Library, University of Rochester; Eric Grunset and Barbara Taylor, at the National Society of the Daughters of the American Revolution; Richard Rose, at the Rochester Museum and Science Center; Susan Crawford, at the National Museum of Natural History; Charles King, at Milne Library, State University of New York at Geneseo; Jerald Pepper, at the Adirondack Museum, Blue Mountain, New York; John and Ray Fadden, at the Six Nations Indian Museum, Onchiota, New York. Steve Love at the Hilles Library helped assist me with the resources of Harvard University's libraries. Kathleen Skelly of the Collections Department opened the Peabody Museum collections of Harvard University while the museum was undergoing renovations. The Rare Books and Manuscripts Division of the New York Public Library and the collections of the Buffalo Historical Society were also useful. A personal inspiration has been John Aubrey at the Newberry Library whose work with captivity narratives is serving so many scholars.

Many thanks to John Drayton of the University of Oklahoma Press for recognizing the import of Jemison and to Sarah I. Morrison for her suggestions for making the edition a more readable work.

The members of my family and my closest friends deserve special gratitude. Additional affection and love go to my sister, Barbara Meltzer; my father, Foster Namias; and to my son, Robert Victor Slavin. They all know how long this edition took. Final thanks go to my mother, Helen Namias, of blessed memory. She was never a captive of Indians, but had a daughter who was. Looking in wonder at the pictures I showed her of whites among Indians she remarked, "You're going back to your childhood!" I knew I was on the right track.

JUNE NAMIAS

Cambridge, Massachusetts

CHRONOLOGY: Key Dates in Mary Jemison's Life

Ca. 1742–43	Birth of Mary Jemison
1756–63	Seven Years' War
1758	Capture by Shawnees; adoption by Senecas
1760	Marriage to Sheninjee
1761	Birth and death of first child
1762	Son Thomas born
	Trek from Ohio to New York
	Death of Sheninjee
Ca. 1762–63	Marriage to Hiokatoo
1766	Birth of John
1776–83	American Revolution
1773	Birth of Nancy
Ca. 1774–77	Birth of Betsey
1779	Sullivan Expedition
1778 or 1779	Birth of Polly
1782	Birth of Jane
1784 or 1785	Birth of Jesse
1811	Death of Thomas
	Death of Hiokatoo
1812	Death of Jesse
1817	Naturalization
1823	Meeting with Seaver
1824	First edition of *A Narrative of the Life of Mrs. Mary Jemison*
1825	Erie Canal completed
1828	Andrew Jackson elected president; re-elected 1832
1833	Death of Mary Jemison

NOTE: Dates on Jemison are my best approximations. Much of this chronology is based on Rev. Charles Delamater Vail's research. Vail finds that Jemison's sequence of events is correct, but her dating of events is off by three years. Using an article in the *Pennsylvania Gazette*, he dates her capture from April 13, 1758. He argues that daughter Polly was born before the Sullivan Expedition (1779) because Jemison fled with five children (*A Narrative of the Life of Mary Jemison: The White Woman of the Genesee . . .* , 21st ed. New York, 1918, pp. 305–7, 310, 346–54, 371, 384, 422–25). I have kept with Jemison's dating of family deaths *after* 1800.

A NARRATIVE OF THE
LIFE OF MRS. MARY JEMISON

EDITOR'S
INTRODUCTION

IN November 1823, a slight woman of about eighty years, walked four miles from her home near Gardeau, by the Genesee River in central New York, to the small cabin of James E. Seaver, a local doctor. For three days she stayed to tell the story of her life. Blue-eyed with a pale complexion, Mary Jemison's hair was grey and slightly curly; her face an expressive one with high cheek bones. When she talked, she held her head down in an Indian manner of humility, "peeping from under her eyebrows." Her clothes, like her life, her demeanor, and her speech, were a blend of cultures: buckskin moccasins, an Indian blanket, a brown flannel gown, a petticoat, and a bonnet. She spoke clearly with "a little of the Irish emphasis" of her origin still recognizable in her voice. Her memory appeared clear to Seaver as he listened to her account. At times, as she spoke of her experiences, tears came to her eyes.[1]

Mary Jemison's story was that of a young immigrant girl captured by Indians; a girl who lost her own family yet gained

---

[1] All references to the Seaver narrative, unless otherwise stated are from James E. Seaver, *A Narrative of the Life of Mrs. Mary Jemison, Who was Taken by the Indians, in the Year 1755, When Only about Twelve Years of Age, and Has Continued to Reside amongst Them to the Present Time* (Canandaigua, N.Y.: J. D. Bemis, 1824). Capitalization of this and all early titles in the notes has been modernized. As to Mary's hair color, Seaver says it was "light chesnut brown," but according to folklore and Mrs. Asher Wright, who saw Mary before her death, it was blonde. *A Narrative of the Life of Mary Jemison: The White Woman of the Genesee*, rev. ed. by Charles Delamater Vail (New York, 1925), hereafter, Seaver, *Life of Mary Jemison* (1925). Vail's notes from Mrs. Asher Wright, 212.

3

4 EDITOR'S INTRODUCTION

a new Seneca family; the story of a white woman who chose
to become an Indian. It is also the story of a woman who
lived through three generations of turmoil in American life,
experiencing change and sorrow—a survivor, an adapter, and
a keen observer.

No copy of Seaver's original notes remains, nor does he
tell us his interviewing technique. What he asked, what he
left out, in what order she chose to tell her story, which are
her words and which his, how she felt about the man from
the world she had left behind to whom she told her story—
these things we cannot know for sure. We do know that
Seaver added pieces to the story as well as an extensive
appendix containing information on Iroquois and Seneca life
and on the American Revolution in western New York.

In 1824, one year after their meeting, Seaver's completed
work, *A Narrative of the Life of Mrs. Mary Jemison, Who was
taken by the Indians, in the year 1755, When only about twelve
years of age, and has continued to reside amongst them to the
present time*, was published in Canandaigua, a small town in
the Finger Lakes region of New York. Over the next 105
years it underwent twenty-seven printings and twenty-three
editions ranging from 32 to 483 pages. First published as an
oddity of local history, known to those in western and central
New York, the books and booklets moved rapidly from rural
New York to second and third printings in London. After
local New York printers issued Seaver's narrative in Batavia,
Auburn, Westfield, Rochester, and Buffalo, the work moved
south for three printings in New York City shortly before the
Civil War. In the late nineteenth century it moved back
across the Atlantic to be printed three times by G. P. Putnam's Sons of London. Thus the remote frontier events told
to Seaver became an internationally known story.[2]

Not only did the narrative gain a wide popular audience,
but it quickly attracted both historical and ethnographic interest. Businessmen, lawyers, anthropologists, and gentleman
historians all became interested in the narrative and in "the
White Woman of the Genesee." Some saw her story as an
ethnographic record of Iroquois and Seneca life. To others

2. Fredrick Strecker, "Tabulation of Editions and Issues of *The Life of Mary
Jemison*," *My First Years as a Jemisonian* (Rochester, 1931).

A NARRATIVE

OF THE LIFE OF

MRS. MARY JEMISON,

Who was taken by the Indians, in the year 1755,
when only about twelve years of age, and
has continued to reside amongst
them to the present time.

CONTAINING

An Account of the Murder of her Father and his
Family; her sufferings; her marriage to two Indians;
her troubles with her Children; barbarities of the
Indians in the French and Revolutionary Wars; the
life of her last Husband, &c.; and many Historical
Facts never before published.
Carefully taken from her own words, Nov. 29th, 1823.

TO WHICH IS ADDED,

An APPENDIX, containing an account of the tragedy
at the Devil's Hole, in 1763, and of Sullivan's Expedition; the Traditions, Manners, Customs, &c. of
the Indians, as believed and practised at the present
day, and since Mrs. Jemison's captivity; together
with some Anecdotes, and other entertaining matter.

BY JAMES E. SEAVER.

CANANDAIGUA:
PRINTED BY J. D. BEMIS AND CO.

1824.

Title page, 1824 Edition. Courtesy of the Rare Books and Special Collections, Rush Rheese Library, University of Rochester.

it was a nonfictional version of *The Last of the Mohicans*, documenting pioneer fortitude and the "decline" of Indian life. During the first sixty years of the twentieth century, variations on the narrative became popular children's books. Early-day national historians referred to Jemison, and in recent years historians and anthropologists have continued to cite the narrative in their histories and studies of early American life and in encyclopedias of Indian life.[3]

CAPTIVITY AND CAPTIVITY NARRATIVES

A Protestant family who left Ireland in 1742 or 1743 to settle in Pennsylvania, the Jemisons were part of a relentless white emigration from the Atlantic coast into the North American forests, mountains, and meadows east of the Mississippi. Whether to find new land for farming or for speculation, the move west was not without risk. As families like the Jemisons moved onto the western Pennsylvania, Maryland, Virginia, and Kentucky frontiers, some of their farms and small villages came under Indian and French attack. Along with the hardships of work on the new frontier, eighteenth-century settlers, like their earlier colonial counterparts, sometimes faced death and capture.[4]

While attacks and captures by Indians were not everyday experiences along the Atlantic and Appalachian frontiers, families could not ignore the potential threat. Accounts of such attacks and captures were well known and contributed to fears and fantasies from the earliest days of colonial settle-

3. Lewis Henry Morgan's edition was James E. Seaver, *Life of Mary Jemison: Deh-he-wä-mis*, 4th ed., with "Geographical and Explanatory Notes" (1856). This edition was reprinted as vol. 41 in the Narratives of North American Indian Captivity series (New York: Garland Publishing, 1977). See also Arthur C. Parker, *The History of the Seneca Indians* (1926; reprint, Port Washington, N.Y.: Ira J. Friedman, 1967); Lois Lenski, *Indian Captive* (1941); James Axtell, "The White Indians of Colonial America," *The European and the Indian* (1981), 168–206 and "The White Indians," in his *The Invasion Within*, 302–27, and James Axtell, ed., "Putting Down the Myth: A Female View," in James Axtell, ed., *The Indian Peoples of Eastern America*, 138–39. Elisabeth Tooker, "The League of the Iroquois: Its History, Politics, and Ritual," in Bruce G. Trigger, ed. *Northeast*, 15:511 in *Handbook of North American Indians*, ed. William C. Sturtevant.

4. Bernard Bailyn, *The Peopling of British North America* and with Barbara De Wolfe, *Voyagers to the West*; Axtell, "The White Indians" in his *The European and the Indian*; Alden T. Vaughan and Daniel K. Richter, "Crossing the Cultural Divide: Indians and New Englanders, 1605–1763"; Alden T. Vaughan and Edward W. Clark, eds., *Puritans among the Indians*.

ment. The population of British America was small—about 2 million in 1763, with a white population of fewer than 200,000 in Pennsylvania and somewhat over 100,000 in New York. Relationships were mostly face-to-face; communication was word of mouth or through the few newspapers and books that circulated. A story of a son, daughter, husband, or wife captured by Indians was big news. Hundreds of captives were taken in the colonial wars between 1675 and 1763. Their stories were the stuff of frontier histories, lore, and fear. The first widely published accounts can be traced back to early New England. In 1676, during King Philip's War, Mary White Rowlandson and other English settlers were captured in a Narragansett Indian attack on Lancaster, Massachusetts. In 1704, during Queen Anne's War, Abenaki Indians and French attacked frontier settlements in southern Maine, New Hampshire, and central Massachusetts. Thirty-eight residents of Deerfield, Massachusetts, were killed; a hundred were captured and taken to Canada. Most, but not all, returned after peace negotiations with the French and Indians. Eunice Williams, the young daughter of Deerfield's Congregational minister, John Williams, did not. She later married and lived the rest of her life with the Catholic Caughnawagas (Mohawks and Oneidas) near Montreal. Mary Rowlandson and John Williams wrote what became widely read narratives of their captivity. Later, with the growth of the popular press and increased literacy, such stories enjoyed continued popularity and were often greatly exaggerated.[5]

Behind the stories that captured American imaginations were the cases of hundreds of Europeans and Americans actually taken prisoner by a variety of tribal groups in North America. In New England alone, an estimated 1,641 white captives were taken between 1675 and 1763. Before 1800, Captain John Smith, Father Isaac Jogues, Mary Rowlandson, Elizabeth Hanson, Hannah Dustin, Eunice Williams, James Smith, Mary Jemison, Frances Slocum, Daniel Boone and his daughter Jemima, all became well-known captives. Eunice Williams, Jemison, and Slocum, along with other, less-famous captives, were adopted into Indian communities. Among the

5. David Hawke, *The Colonial Experience*, 362, 329–331. Population figures for the mid-eighteenth-century colonies are from Gary B. Nash, *The Urban Crucible*, 409. Vaughan and Clark, *Puritans among the Indians*, 31–32.

8   EDITOR'S INTRODUCTION

Senecas, Horatio Jones and Jasper Parrish, both former captives, served as interpreters between whites and Indians.[6]

Far from being a capricious act of a barbarous foe, the taking of captives was an age-old practice around the world. Europeans used capture to acquire labor. In early modern Europe people of the Mediterranean islands were captured and brought to the centers of southern Europe to plant and harvest rice. Africans were captured and enslaved by Europeans, and taken by the millions across the Atlantic for four centuries. Spain, Portugal, France, England, and the Netherlands all participated in this vile system of captivity. Beginning with Columbus's first voyage, Europeans took native peoples from the Western Hemisphere as prisoners, enslaved them, and took them home as novel showpieces of conquest. When Englishmen scouted the North Atlantic in the early 1600s, Indians were frequently abducted and carried to England for future use as guides and interpreters. Squanto of Plymouth was kidnapped in order to be sold into slavery in Spain. His English was learned on board ship and in England. Pocahontas was kidnapped by the early Virginia colonists. After European settlement, capture persisted as a practice of war. For example, hundreds of New England Indians were taken and shipped to the West Indies in the aftermath of King Philip's War (1675–6).[7]

In the Americas, captures had long been an important part of intertribal warfare. In Middle America the Aztecs were feared for their practice of sacrificing enemy captives, while in eastern North America, as we have seen, captivity was a standard tactic of intertribal warfare. Along the St.

6. Vaughan and Richter, "Crossing the Cultural Divide," 23–99. These and other narratives may be found cited in Alden T. Vaughan's bibliography, *Narratives of North American Indian Captivity*. Jasper Parrish became an Indian agent, and Captain Horatio Jones, a former white captive, became an interpreter. Seaver, *Life of Mary Jemison* (1925), from Vail, 157 and 170. See Nancy L. Hagedorn, " 'A Friend to Go Between Them': The Interpreter as Cultural Broker during the Anglo-Iroquois Councils, 1740–70," 60–80.

7. On slavery in Europe see Charles Verlinden, *The Beginnings of Modern Civilization*, chaps. 2 and 3. Neal Salisbury cites several such English raiding expeditions in the early 1600s in *Manitou and Providence*, 90–95. See also David Beers Quinn, *Set Fair for Roanoke*, 356, and *England and the Discovery of America, 1481–1620*, 405–18; James H. Merrell, "The Indians' New World: The Catawba Experience," 537 and 565; Alden T. Vaughan, *New England Frontier*, 3–17; John Donald Duncan, "Indian Slavery"; Carolyn Thomas Foreman, *Indians Abroad, 1493–1938*.

Lawrence River and around the Great Lakes, some of the first European accounts of Indian capture come from the French missionaries working among the Iroquois, Hurons, and Dakotas. These missionaries also reported on the capture and often the torture of enemy warriors and the adoption of women and children. In the struggles for dominance on the North American continent, European and American-born whites and some blacks—priests, soldiers, men, women, and children—were held hostage, adopted, or otherwise incorporated into tribal life.[8]

Capture was rarely an act of caprice. Rather, for Native Americans it was a major strategy of war used against all enemies, regardless of race or culture. Prisoners were taken for four major purposes: to avenge losses of kin, to replace the lost relatives, to prevent expansion onto Indian lands through direct threats to white settlers, and for trade or ransom in exchange for weapons and goods. These purposes were accelerated and magnified with European conquest. Disease and the intense warfare, in which the French, the British, and the Spanish played off one group of Indians against another, left the eastern Woodland Indians of the seventeenth and eighteenth centuries fearing extinction. In parts of the South occasional captures to avenge the loss of kin became a widespread trade in Indian slaves among the Cherokees once trade goods and an entire life-style could be bought by trading the bodies of the enemy. Traditional practice among Iroquois, Hurons, and many other American tribal peoples encouraged the replacement of a dead brother, sister, or spouse by a young person of either sex, who was chosen to become a member of a particular family and was initiated by ritual adoption.[9] Jemison went through such a process, as her narrative recounts.

8. Arthur J. O. Anderson and Charles E. Dibble, trans. and eds., *The War of Conquest*; Reuben Gold Thwaites, ed., *The Jesuit Relations and Allied Documents*.
9. Theda Perdue, *Slavery and the Evolution of Cherokee Society, 1540–1866*, chaps. 1 and 2. See also Richard VanDerBeets, ed., *Held Captive by Indians*, xi; Axtell, *The European and the Indian*, 131–67. On the impact of disease, see Alfred W. Crosby, Jr., *Columbian Exchange*. A different view of captivity as slavery is presented by William A. Starna and Ralph Watkins in "Northern Iroquoian Slavery." Several pieces on captivity as economic servitude appear in Wilcomb E. Washburn, ed., *History of Indian-White Relations*, vol. 4 in Sturtevant, ed., *Handbook of North American Indians*. See "Economic Relations," 404–16.

Narratives like Jemison's are the most comprehensive sources of information concerning the experiences of white captives. Hundreds of them were written between the late seventeenth and early twentieth century. Besides such captivity narratives, the captivity literature included depositions, biographies, oral testimonies, folk histories, newspaper accounts, novels, and dime novels. The captivity genre endured over the entire history of white settlement of each new frontier. Certain themes and actions remained constant; others changed with the time and place, as well as with the sex and age of the captive. Narratives also were affected by the characteristics of the particular Indian group taking prisoners.

The best-selling captivity narratives were about known members of frontier communities, whether recently returned or forever "lost" to Indian or French captors. Some narratives are verifiable in colonial and state records, diaries, sermons, travelers' accounts, newspapers, or military and court records. But for others, our ability to corroborate testimony is hopelessly clouded by folk tales, exaggerations, and the lack of Indian testimony. Still others, like Cooper's captivities in *The Last of the Mohicans*, were pure fiction. Even though the reports of the responses of captives often were influenced by the literary conventions of the period in which they were written, most accounts (at least until the late eighteenth century) were read as real reports of actual, not imagined, situations.

Such historic accounts were among the best-sellers of their day. Mary Rowlandson's *The Sovereignty and Goodness of God* (1682) appeared in thirty editions. John Williams's *The Redeemed Captive Returning to Zion* (1707) sold over 100,000 copies in its first year and was reissued under various titles into its twentieth edition in 1918. Captivity narratives were also popular abroad. Rowlandson's account was first printed simultaneously in London, England, and Cambridge, Massachusetts. Captivity themes also appeared in French and German popular literature during the eighteenth and nineteenth centuries. Even today many popular films such as *The Searchers*, *A Man Called Horse*, *Little Big Man*, *The Emerald Forest*, and most recently, *Dances with Wolves*, depict white children abducted and transformed into Indians.

Why was captivity literature so popular? Why did captivity themes persist? The story of Anglo-American settlement and conquest was one of high drama. It pitted white men and women against the forests, the mountains, and the other natural elements of the North American continent. It was also a drama that scripted white actors against a field of native inhabitants. The outcome of the saga was, for about the first two hundred years, uncertain. In eras lacking film, radio, and television—indeed, when even print was scarce—white men, women, and children in relation to, and often in conflict with, Indians provided the substance of the first and perhaps most lasting of American true stories and tall tales. Scholars have suggested that a propagandistic element aided the continual popularization. Indians were often cast as ready-made savages and contrasted with "civilized" whites. Their "barbarous" actions were used as justification for warfare, expropriation of land, and extermination. Others have pointed to the mythic power that these narratives exerted on a migrating and industrializing culture. Captivity narratives also provided early windows onto Anglo-American, Indian, and French interaction in North America. Besides those functions, captivity stories documented a variety of gender roles in the wilderness. Mary Jemison's account probably was popular because of all of those factors, but as I read her story, it especially touches on issues of gender and ethnicity. Like all women's captivity narratives, it shows a white woman in a near yet foreign world, and in her case, in a world that she learns to accept as her own.[10]

10. Roy Harvey Pearce, "The Significances of the Captivity Narrative" and *Savagism and Civilization*; Richard Slotkin, *Regeneration through Violence* and *The Fatal Environment*; Richard VanDerBeets, "The Indian Captivity Narrative," Ph.d. diss., *Held Captive by Indians*, xi-xxxi, and *The Indian Captivity Narrative*. Other perspectives include James Levernier and Hennig Cohen, eds., *The Indians and Their Captives*, xiii-xxx; Vaughan and Clark, *Puritans among the Indians*, pp. 1–28; Dawn Lander Gherman, "From Parlour to Tepee"; Annette Kolodny, *The Land Before Her*, 3–89; Laurel Thatcher Ulrich, *Good Wives*, 202–14; Pauline Turner Strong, "Captive Images: Stereotypes that Justified Colonial Expansion on the American Frontier Were a Legacy of a Seventeenth-Century War." On popular culture and captivity literature also see Leslie A. Fiedler, "The Indian in Literature in English," in Washburn, ed., *History of Indian-White Relations*, 573–81. For the differences between men's and women's captivity narratives see June Namias, "White Captives: Gender and Ethnicity on Successive American Frontiers, 1607–1862," chaps. 1 and 2 and forthcoming in June Namias, *White Captives*.

Although Jemison's story follows the basic format of the captivity narrative, it differs from most others in three significant respects. Jemison's narrative was one of the first lengthy narratives of Indian captivity in the nineteenth century told by a woman. Others would follow, but none with such authority in terms of years lived with "the enemy." Second, it includes many sympathetic portrayals of Indians and Indian life, which were only occasionally present in earlier examples of the genre. Along with contemporary narratives by male captives Col. James Smith, John Dunn Hunter, and John Tanner, all of whom lived at length with Indians, Jemison's was one of the first to contain considerable and positive information about Indian life.[11] Third, like Rowlandson's and a handful of other narratives, Jemison's remained popular for over a century. For those reasons, reconstructing and rereading her collaboration with Seaver provide insights into early American, nineteenth-century, and Seneca ways of life.

Mary Jemison's narrative stands out among the hundreds of captivity tales because it demonstrates how one woman reacted, interacted, and survived, not for a month or a year, but for a lifetime. Perhaps part of its popularity was due to Jemison's ability to achieve what nineteenth-century American culture could not: an accommodation between two cultures, a womanhood that balanced strength with caring, and an ability to adapt with integrity. Yet her story also contained many familiar elements of the captivity narrative: separation, loss, brutality.

A WHITE WOMAN'S STORY AND AN INDIAN WOMAN'S STORY

The pieces of Mary Jemison's narrative were either told to Seaver or edited by him as a woman's life story. They take us from Mary's girlhood in Pennsylvania and on the Ohio to her marriage and motherhood, through her widowhood and remarriage and the loss of her second husband, to her life as a grandmother and an old woman. The depictions include her capture, her integration into a new community, her work in that community, her trials as a mother, and her observations

11. See these works fully cited in Vaughan, *Narratives of North American Indian Captivity.*

in her later years as she looks back over her life. In its progression and in those contexts, the work reflects what Joyce Antler calls a woman's life course. As such it is part of the larger body of biography, autobiography, and fiction about women's lives that provided popular reading in nineteenth-century America.[12]

Mary Jemison was born on board ship in 1742 or 1743. Her Scotch-Irish parents, Thomas Jemison and Jane Erwin Jemison, settled on a farm in western Pennsylvania about ten miles north of present-day Gettysburg. On April 5, 1758, when Mary was about fifteen, the Jemison family and visiting friends were attacked by Shawnee and French forces. Mary's parents, two brothers, a sister, and the visitors were killed. Only she and the friends' young boy were spared. Her Shawnee captors carried the terrified girl down the Ohio River.[13] She recognized her mother's red hair as she watched them dry, clean, and paint scalps. Near Fort Duquesne (later Fort Pitt) on the Monongahela, she was given to two Seneca women.

Jemison's story was similar to those of many young male and female captives of the Iroquois nations, but few gave a detailed account of their experiences. Like all captives among the Iroquois, Mary was claimed by bereaved women who would decide her fate. Arriving at their village, she was washed, cleaned, and dressed "Indian style." The two Seneca

12. Joyce Antler, *Lucy Sprague Mitchell: The Making of a Modern Woman*. For a detailed analysis see Namias, "White Captives," chap. 5. Three works of criticism that informed my analysis of Jemison's narrative as a white woman's story are Elaine Showalter, ed., *Feminist Criticism*; Nina Baym, *Woman's Fiction*; and Ann Douglas, *Feminization of American Culture*.

13. In the *Narrative*, Mary says her capture was in 1755, but a *Philadelphia Gazette* account of April 13, 1758, puts the date in early April of that year. See Vail's notes in Seaver, *Life of Mary Jemison* (1925), with a facsimile of the newspaper article opposite page 128 and discussion, pp. 314–17. Vail indicates that all of Jemison's dating is three years off. Her dates after 1800 appear to be more accurate. Regarding the Jemison family's departure, Vail says the ship, *William and Mary*, sailed from Belfast and arrived in Philadelphia on October 6, 1743, but indicates another possible voyage with an arrival in Philadelphia in late December, 1742, or early January, 1743. He suggests that the Jemison family had the means to avoid such a winter trip, and in the interest of "preserving the integrity and dignity of the Mary Jemison legend" opts for the October, 1743, date. The actual date appears to have fallen between October, 1742, and January, 1743; see pp. 309–11, and Eleanor Robinette Dobson, "Mary Jemison," *Dictionary of American Biography*, 10, (New York, 1933), 10:39–40. On Shawnee life see R. David Edmunds, *The Shawnee Prophet*, and Charles Callender, "Shawnee," in Trigger, ed., *Northeast*, 622–35.

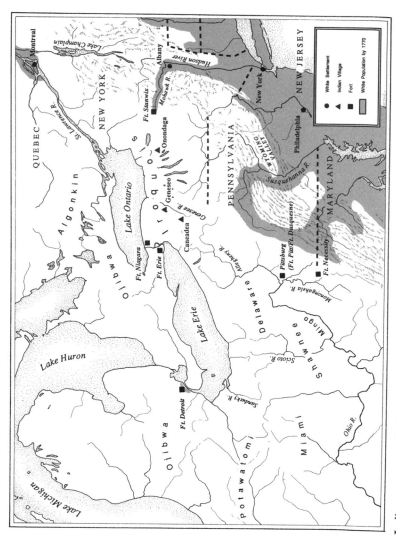

Indian country and the western frontier; 1755–75

sisters had lost their brother in battle the year before. As Mary sat with them, many women of the village came into the wigwam and mourned: "all the Squaws in the town came in to see me. I was soon surrounded by them, and they immediately set up a most dismal howling, crying bitterly, and wringing their hands in all the agonies of grief for a deceased relative."[14]

Then one stepped forward and, "in a voice somewhat between speaking and singing," recounted the life of the dead brother, his qualities, the situation of his death, and fate of his spirit now risen to " 'the land of his fathers.' " But soon Mary became the focus of their attention and their joy. They renamed her and substituted her for the lost brother. Through this ritual adoption, she said, "I was ever considered and treated by them as a real sister, the same as though I had been born of their mother."[15]

With peace negotiations ending the Seven Years' War in 1763, Mary, like other prisoners of war, was to be returned to the British. She was taken to Fort Pitt and talked with Englishmen there. But her new sisters resisted her return: "believing that I should be taken from them, [they] hurried me into their canoe and recrossed the river—took their bread out of the fire and fled with me, without stopping. . . . They

14. See 76 below.
15. Pp. 76–78 below. Daniel K. Richter, "War and Culture: The Iroquois Experience," 528–59, and "Iroquois versus Iroquois: Jesuit Missions and Christianity in Village Politics, 1642–1686." For the replacement of population through war (called "Mourning War"), see Richter, "Ordeals of the Longhouse," in Daniel K. Richter and James II. Merrell, eds., *Beyond the Covenant Chain*, 11–39. Tom Cook reminded me that not only Jemison herself but all of her children probably were given Seneca names by the clan mothers at the Midwinter or the Green Corn ceremony; however, I found no record of these. Correspondence, Tom Cook, December 7, 1988. Seaver says Jemison's new name was Dickewamis, meaning "a pretty girl, a handsome girl or a pleasant, good thing." Arthur C. Parker claims that no such construction exists in Seneca, and says her name was Dehgewanus, meaning the sound of falling voices. The folklore and various editions, however, hold to Dickewamis and the childlike and romantic meaning of the name. In the National Museum of Natural History's copy of the 1856 New York edition, *Life of Mary Jemison: Deh-he-wä-mis*, Iroquois ethnographer J. N. B. Hewitt penned in a correction to Morgan's subtitle: "De-gi-wa-'ne n's ='Two women's voices falling,' " and signed, "Hewitt." William N. Fenton suggests "Two-voices-falling or Two falling voices," citing Clara Redeye, July 18, 1934. Fenton writes her name as Degiwene's, "Two-voices falling" or "Two falling voices" (correspondence, December 3, 1988). In these two cases and others here I have left out the more technical linguistic markings.

never once stopped rowing till they got home."[16] Her feelings were mixed. She had been with the Senecas for over a year. She says that, although "the sight of white people who could speak English inspired me with an unspeakable anxiety to go home with them, and share in the blessings of civilization" and her sisters' actions "seemed like a second captivity," after much brooding she gradually became "as contented as before."[17]

At this time, the Delawares lived with some Senecas on the Ohio. Her sisters arranged her marriage to a Delaware. "Not daring to cross them, or disobey their commands, with a great degree of reluctance I went; and Sheninjee and I were married according to Indian custom." Remembering him, she said:

> Sheninjee was a noble man; large in stature; elegant in his appearance; generous in his conduct; courageous in war; a friend to peace, and a great lover of justice. He supported a degree of dignity far above his rank, and merited and received the confidence and friendship of all the tribes with whom he was acquainted. Yet, Sheninjee was an Indian. The idea of spending my days with him, at first seemed perfectly irreconcilable to my feelings: but his good nature, generosity, tenderness, and friendship towards me, soon gained my affection; and, strange as it may seem, I loved him!—To me he was ever kind in sickness, and always treated me with gentleness; in fact, he was an agreeable husband, and a comfortable companion.[18]

Two years later, attended by her sisters, she gave birth to her first child. The girl died after two days.[19] Jemison suffered another loss when she heard of Sheninjee's death. When she remarried, her choice was Hiokatoo (Big Lance), a much older man and a respected Seneca warrior. During the fourth year of her captivity she gave birth to her first son, naming him after her father, Thomas Jemison.

16. P. 80 below. For the account of a white captive married to Oneida chief Thomas King who resisted return to white society see William M. Beauchamp, *A History of the New York Iroquois*, New York State Museum, Bulletin 78 (Albany, 1905), p. 319.

17. Pp. 80–81 below.

18. P. 82 below. See Ives Goddard, "Delaware," in Trigger, ed., *Northeast*, 213–39.

19. P. 82 below.

As the years went by, Jemison tells us, her "anxiety to get away, to be set at liberty, and leave them, had almost subsided. With them was my home; my family was there, and there I had many friends to whom I was warmly attached in consideration of the favors, affection and friendship with which they had uniformly treated me, from the time of my adoption."[20]

After the Revolutionary War she was again offered a chance to return to the white world. Her eldest son, Thomas, "was anxious" for her to leave, but she had married Hiokatoo in 1765 and had six more children. She refused to return to white society, fearing that such relatives as she might still have left would reject her Indian children: "they would despise them, if not myself; and treat us as enemies: or, at least with a degree of cold indifference, which I thought I could not endure."[21]

Here and throughout the narrative, Jemison appeals to her audience in a call to recognize her dilemmas as a woman and as a white woman between two cultures. But Jemison's narrative moves from those problems to describe the life of one who accepts her new culture and becomes a Seneca woman. Any evaluation of Jemison as an Indian woman (which is what she chose to remain) must come to terms with the old images and negative views of Indian women before we can examine the Seneca world in which she lived.

The view of Indian women held by the first Europeans went beyond the dual image, either savage or noble, that Europeans had of Indians in general. A third image emerged at first contact depicting an exotic and sexual native. First pictures of the Americas represented the hemisphere as home to bare-breasted native women. The presumed easy sexuality of the woman of the Americas was represented during the Spanish Conquest by Malinche (renamed Dona Marina), the Indian translator, diplomat, and lover of Cortés. In English lore, the nubile, beautiful, sexually free and available native woman was Pocahontas, first presented by John Smith. On the savage theme, Theodor de Bry's first European drawings of America illustrated women's supposedly savage features

20. P. 83 below.
21. Pp. 119–20 below.

by showing bestial women with sagging breasts chopping up
"innocent" European explorers and tossing them into cooking
pots. In the *Jesuit Relations*, women (along with men) became
the coperpetrators of violence against French Catholic and
enemy Indian prisoners. James Axtell's research on French
and English white captives entering Indian villages reported
women and children throwing things and hitting the captives
with "ax handles, tomahawks, hoop poles, clubs, and
switches" as they ran the gauntlet, "as if to beat the whiteness
out of them."[22]

Eighteenth- and nineteenth-century North American
sources often depicted Indian women as inferior drudges who
dragged around heavy loads and did most of the work while
Indian men lolled about and had a good time. These women
were viewed as little more than slaves with no political power,
and no skills worth mentioning. An equally negative but
opposite position was held by an eighteenth-century Mora-
vian missionary to the Delaware, John Heckewelder, who
concluded that women's work in the fields lasted for six
months while men's work was "year round." He called wom-
en's work "not hard or difficult," claiming that their indoor
work was "very trifling" and their agricultural work "periodical and of short duration" while their husbands' work was
"constant and severe in the extreme. . . . Of his exertions as
a hunter, their [family's] existence depends."[23]

Recent scholars have challenged earlier myths that wom-
en's work was either drudgery or unimportant.[24] Closer atten-

22. Gary Nash, "Red, White, and Black: The Origins of Racism in Colonial
America," in Gary B. Nash and Richard Weiss, eds., *The Great Fear*, 1–2. See also
Rayna Green, "The Pocahontas Perplex: The Image of Indian Women in American
Culture"; Hugh Honour, *New Golden Land*; Octavio Paz, *Labyrinth of Solitude*, trans.
Lysander Kemp; On Smith see Edward Arber and A. G. Bradley, eds., *Travels
and Works of Captain John Smith*; Mary V. Dearborn, *Pocahontas's Daughters*; and
Namias, "White Captives," chaps. 2 and 3. Representations of Indian women
are found in Bernadette Bucher, *Icon and Conquest*. For one Jesuit example see,
"Captivity of Father Isaac Jogues, of the Society of Jesus, among the Mohawks,"
in VanDerBeets, *Held Captive*, 13–15. The quotation from Axtell, "The White
Indians of Colonial America," is in Axtell, *European and the Indian*, 184–86.
23. John Heckewelder, *History, Manners, and Customs of the Iroquois Nations
Who Once Inhabited Pennsylvania and the Neighboring States*, 154–55 and 158–59.
24. Patricia Albers and Beatrice Medicine, *The Hidden Half*; Sylvia Van Kirk,
Many Tender Ties. The Iroquoian collections at Harvard University's Peabody
Museum, the Rochester (New York) Museum and Science Center, and the National
Museum of Natural History in the Smithsonian Institution gave me a sense of native

tion to the art and crafting of clothing, tools, and dwellings has also brought greater respect for Indian women's skills. Examples of Iroquois brooches, dresses, quilled knife holders, floral designed purses, moccasins, and deerskin leggings, show how native women of Jemison's era combined the practical, the spiritual, and the aesthetic. The narrow vision of the early Europeans and Americans (usually males) was often distorted by their culture's view of others, and their own preconceptions of gender roles. It appears that many Euro-Americans were blind to, or deliberately obscured, the nature of Indian societies for personal, religious, and political reasons.[25]

Among students of the Iroquois, women figure in this wider debate which goes back at least to the mid-nineteenth century. The "father of anthropology," Lewis Henry Morgan, claimed that "the Indian regarded women as the inferior, the dependent, and the deviant of man, and from nurture and habit, she actually considered herself to be." On the other hand, Harriet Maxwell Converse, who worked and lived among the Iroquois in the late nineteenth century, found that women had significant roles in kinship, marriage, child rearing, politics, religious life, and agriculture.[26]

Clearly both sexes were needed. That truth is implicit in Jemison's narrative and in Iroquoian cosmology as well. In the Iroquoian world view, human life was created when one of the Ancient Ones was pushed through a hole in the sky-world. As she fell, the birds, fishes, and amphibians below

artistry. Also see Axtell, *Indian Peoples of Eastern America; A Documentary History of the Sexes.*

25. Perdue, *Slavery and the Evolution of Cherokee Society,* pp. 9 and 11, and "Amerindian Women: Old World Perceptions, New World Realities," lecture, Harvard University, March 8, 1988. Tzvetan Todorov, *Conquest of America;* Eleanor Burke Leacock, *Myths of Male Dominance.*

26. Lewis H. Morgan, *League of the Ho-dé-no-sau-nee or Iroquois,* 1, 315; Harriet Maxwell Converse, *Myths and Legends of the New York State Iroquois,* esp. "Women's Rights among the Iroquois," p. 139. The debate on Iroquois women goes on: see Judith K. Brown, "Iroquois Women: An Ethnohistoric Note," in Rayna R. Reiter, ed., *Toward an Anthropology of Women,* 235–51, and Elisabeth Tooker, "Women in Iroquois Society," in Michael K. Foster et. al., eds., *Extending the Rafters,* 109–23, esp. 112–15. Brown takes the economic position. Tooker minimizes women's power, pointing out that matrilineal kinship and matrilocal patterns of residence among the Iroquois were frequently found among other Indians in North America and do not necessarily indicate an improved social status. For more on this debate see in Rayna Green's, *Native American Women: A Bibliography,* under "Iroquois."

showed their concern and conferred to find a way to save her. Muskrat dove into the sea and came up with earth to place on Turtle's back. From here the woman gave birth to twin boys and brought corn and the means of subsistence to the growing earth on Turtle's back.[27]

The Senecas, or Onotowa-ka (pron. Onnn-no-do-wa'ga or Onun-duwa-ga, "people of the hills" or "people of the big hill"), were a matrilineal, agriculturally based people living in cleared settlements in the western parts of what is now New York state and southwest into Ohio. Like all of the Iroquois, their lives were dictated by seasonal cycles. Their sense of time ran not by the clock but by a lunar calendar in which the name of each moon told the nature of earth, the animals, and the spirits at that time of year: Moon of Long Nights, Starving Moon, Maple Moon, Frog Moon, Planting Moon, Strawberry Moon, Moon of Green Corn, Corn Harvest Moon, and Moon of Falling Leaves.[28] Jemison remembers her first years along the Ohio: in springtime through late fall, her village lived along the river; after harvest, they moved inland to their winter camp, where the men would hunt and trap beaver. When she moved north to live in Seneca country, she recalled her first child's birth when "the kernels of corn first appeared on the cob."

Among the Seneca, women had extensive power. Along with men they possessed the knowledge of and were involved with the medical cures. Politically, economically, and socially, women's powers, women's words, and the works of their hands were respected. Although women's powers apparently diminished in the later years of Jemison's life because

27. J. N. B. Hewitt, "Iroquoian Cosmology," pt. 1, *Twenty-first Annual Report of the Bureau of American Ethnology*, 221–28. On Iroquois ritual, see Elisabeth Tooker, ed., *An Iroquois Source Book*, vol. 3.

28. My spelling of Onotowa-ka is a simplification of the linguistic spelling suggested by Ives Goddard, with the pronunciations based on conversations with Allegany Seneca Myrtle Peterson and anthropologist William N. Fenton. Cadwallader Colden used "Senekas" and "Sennekas" in *The History of the Five Indian Nations Depending on the Province of New-York in America* (1727 and 1747). The Senecas' Iroquois Council name means "the doorkeeper": they are the keepers of the western door of the Iroquois League. See Thomas S. Abler and Elisabeth Tooker, citing Ives Goddard, in "Seneca," in Trigger, ed., *Northeast*, 513–14. For linguistically correct spellings and suggested pronunciations, see Wallace L. Chafe, *Handbook of the Seneca Language*. Joseph Bruchac provided me with this Iroquois calendar in a telephone conversation, January 9, 1988.

of military defeat in the American Revolution, the movement onto reservations, and the coming of a Seneca millennial movement, they were formidable during most of her lifetime. They included the "power of life and death over prisoners of war," the choice of male members to sit in the councils of war, the ability to remove council members if they did not comply with the wishes of the clan mothers, the selection of and participation in the leadership of tribal spiritual life, the passing of property and titles through the female line, the arrangement of marriages and the authority over the extended and extensive household, the longhouse. The traditional longhouse was composed of many related families and had up to fifty or sixty residents. Seneca men hunted and fished and were involved in the far-flung organization of diplomacy and warfare. Their power was great, but it was shared with women. Even labor, often cited as being rigidly divided between Indian men and women, was not so among the Senecas. Mary Jemison talks of how she went out on the hunt, where she was responsible for cleaning skins and bringing them back to the village.[29]

Seneca women had full responsibility for the planting, gathering, and harvesting that was critical to community survival. In western New York the snow comes early and the winters are long and severe. In deep snows and cold weather it is difficult to hunt, and tracking game is an uncertain enterprise. Hunting, when successful, provided needed protein and variety in the Seneca diet, but crops gathered and stored in underground caches for the winter were a significant and often a more predictable part of the diet from December through March.

Concurring but differing with conventional discussions of Indian women's work, Jemison said her labor was "not severe." Comparing white and Indian women, she said of the Seneca "their task is probably not harder than that of white women . . . and their cares certainly are not half as numerous, nor as great." Seneca women planted in the late spring with short-handled hoes. Recalling her summers in Ohio, Jemison

29. Anthony F. C. Wallace, *The Death and Rebirth of the Seneca*; George S. Snyderman, *Behind the Tree of Peace*; William N. Fenton, "Northern Iroquoian Culture Patterns," in Trigger, ed., *Northeast*, 300–3; Joan Jensen, "Native American Women and Agriculture: A Seneca Case Study." See 84 below.

said "we planted, tended and harvested our corn, and generally had all our children with us; but had no master to oversee or drive us, so that we could work as leisurely as we pleased."[30]

A world of seasonal cycles was the ongoing continuity of Seneca life. The foods women planted were called the "Three Sisters," "Our Supporters," "Our Life": corn, beans, and squash. In the spring of the year the Seneca people gathered (as they still gather) for the Green Corn Festival. On the first day of that festival an incantation was given to the Great Spirit. Thanks were said for preserving the people, and recognition and thanks were given for the ceremony itself "descended to us from our fathers": "Great Spirit, continue to listen: We thank thee for thy great goodness in causing our mother, the earth, again to bring forth her fruits. . . . (Throwing on tobacco). Preserve us from all danger. Preserve our aged men. Preserve our mothers. Preserve our warriors. Preserve our children."[31] These seasonal prayers were probably heard by Jemison and her children. Both mothers and fathers, the principles of maleness and femaleness, were recognized. Such a balance of power and recognition of both principles showed respect for both.[32]

From her Scotch-Irish tradition, Jemison remembered, and showed respect for, both sexes in her own family, naming her children after her father, her mother, her sisters, and her brothers. Along with raising children, Jemison's new culture recognized women's closeness to the sacred forces, their importance in growing food, in providing clothing, in governing, and in war. During Jemison's lifetime Seneca women had rights possessed by few women in white or black America.

SENECA AND NORTH AMERICAN CONTEXTS

Mary Jemison's life was a long one lived in times of great change. The best estimates put her birth in 1743, her death

---

30. P. 84 below.
31. Morgan, *League of . . . Iroquois*, 1: 153, 192. J. N. B. Hewitt, "A Constitutional League of Peace in the Stone Age of America: The League of the Iroquois and Its Constitution," *Annual Report of the Smithsonian Institution for 1918*, 527–45, in Tooker, ed. *An Iroquois Source Book: Political and Social Organization*, 1:543–45.
32. Iroquois religious beliefs went through many changes in this time. On Fenton's concept of "upstreaming," that is arguing back from present practice to earlier usages, see Daniel K. Richter, "Up the Cultural Stream: Three Recent Works in Iroquois Studies."

in 1833—a life of ninety years.[33] At the time of Mary's birth and capture, France and Spain controlled vast empires; Britain's colonies hugged a narrow strip of the Atlantic shore. Much of the Ohio valley, the upper Mississippi valley, and what is now southeastern Canada were claimed by France, but these were homelands of the League of the Six Nations, Iroquois, along with the Delawares, the Shawnees, the Ojibwas, the Hurons, the Dakotas, and other indigenous peoples. Spain claimed Florida, the rest of the Gulf Coast, and the area west of the Mississippi, including all of Mexico. By the time Jemison was twenty, the political map of North America was radically transformed. With the defeat of the French by British forces in Quebec in 1763, the French missions, traders, forts, and communities came under British control.

The Proclamation Line of 1763 represented Britain's attempt to keep its promises to Iroquois and other Indian allies by restricting white settlement east of the Appalachians. But British policy on the frontier failed to separate whites from Indians, and by 1775 antagonism was rife. As the opening shots at Lexington and Concord marked the onset of the Revolution in the east, shots between a variety of Woodland Indians and backcountry settlers and speculators defined the Revolution on the western border. North American tribal groups were forced to side with the Crown or the newly emerging rebels. Four of the Six Nations of the Iroquois sided with the British; two, the Oneidas and the Tuscaroras, allied themselves with the rebelling colonists. When the new United States successfully emerged, the Mohawks, the Onondagas, the Senecas, and the Cayugas were treated as defeated enemies. At the close of the War of Independence, white settlers pushed their way brazenly, and not without bloodshed, into Kentucky, the Ohio valley and western New York and Pennsylvania. Between 1808 and 1836—under the administrations of Madison, Monroe, Adams, and Jackson—New York, which since the sixteenth century had been dominated by the Iroquois League, was transformed by the introduction of

---

33. Seaver, *A Narrative of the Life of Mrs. Mary Jemison*, intro. by Allen W. Trelease (1975), viii; and "Mary Jemison," in Edward T. James et al., eds., *Notable American Women, 1607–1950*, 2:271–73.

canals, state roads, market agriculture, new townships, cities, industry, and millennial religion.[34] What could these changes have meant to the native peoples whose ancestors had lived in the lands from the Hudson valley to the banks of Lake Erie, Lake Ontario, and beyond? What could they have meant to Jemison herself, who, although an immigrant child from a frontier family, lived for many decades among these people?

Contrary to lore, popular fiction, and film, Iroquois people were not continually running through the forest carrying hatchets. Calling themselves the Ho-de-no-sau-nee (pronounced Ho-de'no-saw-nee), meaning "People of the Longhouse," the Six Nations of the Iroquois Confederacy were powerful in their own right. Before log cabins replaced them in the mid to late eighteenth century, the longhouses were the center of Iroquois family life and also provided the actual as well as the symbolic bases of Iroquois government and society. Numerous nuclear families were present, each with its own fire and platforms on either side for sleeping. A representation of the clan ancestor was affixed to the gables, and throughout the Six Nations hospitality was extended to visiting clan members, all of whom were seen as kin. At marriage, a husband would move into his wife's (really his mother-in-law's) residence although he kept his mother's clan affiliation for life. His children were members of his wife's clan, and in the case of divorce they remained with her. The departing husband and father had to take his personal belongings with him and either return into his mother's house or move into the household of a new wife.[35]

Language, culture, and history divided Iroquoian-speaking peoples from their Algonquian-speaking neighbors on the north and east, and their Dakota-speaking neighbors farther west. Household and village life was based on kin relationships. Members of each household were seen as descendants

34. Barbara Graymont, *The Iroquois in the American Revolution*, 101–8 and 142–56; Paul E. Johnson, *A Shopkeepers' Millennium*; Robert L. Heilbroner and Aaron Singer, *The Economic Transformation of America*, 88–124.

35. Pronunciation from Myrtle Peterson, Ho-DI'-no-saw-ni, alternatively Ho-de-no-shawy-ni, suggested by William N. Fenton, telephone conversation, January 9, 1989. Arthur C. Parker, "An Analytical History of the Seneca Indians" and *The Indian How Book*; Elisabeth Tooker, ed., *An Iroquois Source Book* and *Calendric Rituals*, vol. 3; and Wallace, *Death and Rebirth*, chaps. 3 and 4.

of clan mothers, who in turn were distantly related to a common animal ancestor. Turtle, Bear, Wolf, Snipe, Heron, and Deer were all Seneca ancestors—the first three and some of the others were clans throughout Iroquois territory. Elder women in the household provided the closest link to the ancient ancestor. Because Mary Jemison was a captive, she was adopted into her Seneca sisters' and mother's clan, which appears to have been either Heron or Turtle.[36]

Religion, politics, and kinship thus worked, in the seventeenth and eighteenth centuries, to unify highly localized and widely separated villages. According to their traditions, Iroquoian-speaking peoples had a history of internal warfare. Around 1450 a prophet named Deganawidah, "the Peacemaker," united the warring nations between the Hudson River and the Great Lakes. He travelled over the countryside to bind up these nations' wounds. Gaining the confidence of the people, he forged an alliance of the five nations under the Tree of Peace. The territory of the five nations of the longhouse began where the sun rose in the east among the Mohawks in the Mohawk valley and extended to the Oneidas, the Onondagas, and the Cayugas in central New York and around the Finger Lakes setting in Seneca country. The Senecas were the People of the Western Door: their lands included the area along Lake Ontario and Lake Erie and south to the Allegheny River. Thus was formed the Great League of Peace of the Iroquois Confederacy, or Ganonhsyoni, the "Lodge Extended Lengthwise." During the late seventeenth century the confederacy made a system of alliances with the British known as the Covenant Chain. Members of the five nations were designated to represent both clan and nation. They met annually at what became known as the Grand Council at Onondaga. Representatives of the clans went through ceremonial exchanges and rituals of mourning and

36. This composite description of early kin and longhouse life was drawn from many anthropological and ethnohistorical sources including Morgan, Hewitt, Beauchamp, Converse, Parker, Fenton, Brown, Tooker, Wallace, and Graymont. Also see Frank Gouldsmith Speck, *The Iroquois*. Jemison never mentions either clan, and Seaver does not seem to have asked. Later correspondence of her descendents mentions both the Huron and the Turtle clans. See the William Prior Letchworth Collection maintained by the Genesee State Park Region at Castile, N.Y., and Milne Library, SUNY at Geneseo, N.Y.; Tom Cook, "The Letchworth Collection: A Survey of a 19th Century Indian Museum."

consolation for lost members, and met to coordinate policy. The Tuscaroras became the sixth nation of the confederacy when, after their defeat by North Carolina whites between 1711 and 1713, they fled north and were adopted by the Oneidas.[37]

Their reputation as tireless and intransigent warriors made the Iroquois leading political contenders in North America during the seventeenth and eighteenth centuries. In the seventeenth century they waged war against the Hurons in Canada for control of the beaver trade and to replenish their shrinking population. In the first half of the eighteenth century the Iroquois's power and geopolitical position made them sought after by both the British and the French. Wise to their position, the confederacy played off British against French for more than half a century, reaping trade goods, weapons, and other benefits from each side. Their power was further advanced when Iroquois men fanned out over the Ohio country, building alliances with Shawnees, Delawares, Miamis, and tribes as far south as the Carolinas.[38]

By the mid-eighteenth century increasing international pressures along with long-standing local divisions within the confederacy, including religious and trade affiliations with both French and English, made neutrality difficult to maintain. During the Seven Years' War (1756-1763), Mohawks supported the British, and Senecas often sided with the French. At the close of the war French control in North America ended. British moves to dominate the Ohio country, along with an inability to halt white settlement, brought the

37. Paul A. W. Wallace, *The White Roots of Peace*. Deganawidah revealed his mission to Hiawatha, whose "eloquence persuaded the people and the chiefs to lay aside the blood feud and unite." A. F. C. Wallace, *Death and Rebirth*, 94–98. On the Tuscaroras' relationship with the Oneidas, see Barbara Graymont, "The Oneidas and the American Revolution," in Jack Campisi and Laurence M. Hauptman, eds., *The Oneida Indian Experience*. For maps of Iroquois and Great Lakes Indians, see Helen Hornbeck Tanner, ed., *Atlas of Great Lakes Indian History*.

38. Allen W. Trelease, *Indian Affairs in Colonial New York*; Bruce G. Trigger, *The Children of Aataentsic*; A. F. C. Wallace, *Death and Rebirth*, 111 and chap. 5. For more on Iroquois history in colonial America see Colden, *The History of the Five Indian Nations*. Recent analyses include Francis Jennings, *The Ambiguous Iroquois Empire* and *Empire of Fortune*, and Richter and Merrell, eds., *Beyond the Covenant Chain*. For source materials see Francis Jennings, William N. Fenton, et al., eds., *History and Culture of Iroquois Diplomacy: An Interdisciplinary Guide to the Treaties of the Six Nations and Their League*.

Iroquois into an alliance with Ohio-country tribes and ultimately into a conflict known as Pontiac's Rebellion (1763).
This collective attempt to stay British power proved unsuc-
cessful, and it was an indicator of the limitations of the old
neutral, play-off diplomacy. After the first Treaty of Stanwix
(1768) the Iroquois were caught between the demands of their
southern and western Indian allies, the British, and the ever-
increasing appetites for land of white frontier settlers.[39]

As the rift between the mother country and colonial British subjects deepened in 1775, the Six Nations realized it was
in their best interest to stay out of what they saw as a family
quarrel. Yet, in negotiating with the newly forming government of the colonies, they insisted that their territories not
be used to pass through and attack British positions. With
increasing hostilities, such requests were not taken seriously.
In September, 1776, at Oswego the confederacy council met,
their women were consulted, and four of the six Iroquois
nations declared their support for Britain. The New York
and Pennsylvania backcountry soon became a theater of war
with Iroquoia one of its first casualties. The first engagement
at Oriskany (August, 1777) cost both sides, but the Senecas
lost thirty-six warriors; another thirty-eight were wounded.
Mary Jemison reported, "our town exhibited a scene of real
sorrow and distress when our warriors returned."[40]

Even as ways changed, nature as much as politics determined the lives the Ho-de-no-sau-nec. If hostilities were
called for, the summer and fall months were appropriate
times. As late as 1777, Iroquois forces left the fall battlefield
for the hunt. The food needed to sustain their families in the
winter came first. In the spring they resumed fighting.[41] But
within the next three years Iroquois country and the northern
Pennsylvania settlements were turned successively by one
side then the other into parched earth; old ways were chipped
away. The divisions between Revolutionary-allied Oneidas
and Tuscaroras and the four Iroquois nations allied with Loyalist and British forces sharpened during the war. By 1779
and 1780, Oneida towns were attacked by Joseph Brant, the

39. Wallace, *Death and Rebirth*, 114–23.
40. See p. 100 below.
41. Wallace, *Death and Rebirth*, 136.

leading Mohawk supporter of Britain. Combined Loyalist, British, and Iroquois attacks on the Wyoming, Cherry Valley, and German Flats settlements resulted in the burning of hundreds of square miles of farmland; the destruction of farms, cattle, and sheep; and in the first two cases, the deaths of settlers and taking of women and children as prisoners (most of whom were released shortly thereafter). One Cherry Valley prisoner told Mary Jemison how she and her three daughters had been taken prisoner. In their case, like that of the Jemison family's, a lack of preparation had brought on disaster. After Cherry Valley, fear and destruction, along with atrocity stories, gave rise to demands for a ferocious assault on the British, and especially their allied Indian forces. The result galvanized the Sullivan Expedition, a fighting force of three thousand men whose mission forever transformed the course of Iroquois and Seneca life.[42]

Corn was such a determinant of tribal existence that both the French empire builders and the American Revolutionaries tried to decimate Iroquois power not on the battlefield as much as in the cornfield. Seventeenth- and eighteenth-century sources show the great admiration of Europeans from Champlain onward for Iroquois fields of grain. As far back as 1687, New France's governor-general, the Marquis de Denonville, had "deemed it our best policy to employ ourselves laying the Indian corn which is in vast abundance in the fields, rather than to follow a flying enemy to a distance and excite our troops to catch only some straggling fugitives." According to Arthur C. Parker, French reports had time in four Seneca villages "spent in destroying the corn which was in such great abundance that the loss including old corn which was in the cache which we burnt and that which was standing, was computed according to the estimate afterwards made at 400 thousand minots (about 1,200,000 bushels) of Indian corn."[43]

42. See p. 99 below. Vail says the Cherry Valley mother was Mrs. John Moore, who was captured on November 11, 1778, along with Mrs. Jane Campbell. Campbell's four children and others were taken to Kanadesaga (Geneva), where all were released a year later. Vail's notes, "Cherry Valley Captives," in Seaver, *Life of Mary Jemison* (1925), 395–96. Wallace, *Death and Rebirth*, 130–44; Graymont, *Iroquois and the American Revolution*, 136–39.

43. Parker cites the early colonial French sources, Pierre F. X. de Charlevoix

Mary Jemison was in her thirties when this tactic of cutting or burning the corn fields was taken up by Sullivan's Continental army in south-central and western New York. In a report to General Washington on September 16, 1779, Daniel Brodhead wrote regarding an attack on Seneca farms along the Allegheny that the "troops remained on the ground three whole days destroying the Towns & Corn Fields." In a September 30, 1779, letter to John Jay, an officer of Major General John Sullivan wrote of his success with this policy. Along with burning five major towns in "Cayuga country," Colonel Butler boasted that he had "destroyed two hundred acres of excellent corn with a number of orchards one of which had in it 1500 fruit trees." Besides laying waste to another forty towns, Butler's troops ruined corn amounting to 160,000 bushels "at a modest computation," "along with a vast quantity of vegetables of every kind." Continued Butler, "I flatter myself that the orders with which I was entrusted are fully executed, as we have not left a single settlement or a field of corn in the country of the Five Nations." Jemison's recollections of the devastation struck by American troops in Seneca country are more realistic and less heroic in their view of the Revolutionary cause.[44]

In the first years after the Sullivan invasion Seneca families died of starvation and disease. Others fled to British forts for support. Jemison took her family and worked as a tenant farmer on the lands of two runaway slaves. Later, with the land settlement that gave her the Gardeau tract, Jemison, her husband, and her sons and daughters farmed the rich Genesee valley land.

The years following the Revolution hardly brought the benevolent gifts of republicanism to Iroquoia. Rather, the scourge of war left permanent scars. The Great League of Peace, split by civil war during the Revolution, remained divided in its aftermath. Seventy-eight Mohawks and other Iroquois moved with Joseph Brant to Grand River in Ontario,

and Louis Armand de Lom d'Arce de Lahontan, but calls these figures an overestimation. Arthur C. Parker, "Iroquois Uses of Maize and Other Food Plants," in William N. Fenton, *Parker on the Iroquois*, 18.
    44. Fenton, *Parker on the Iroquois*, 19–20, citing *Journals of the Military Expedition of Major General John Sullivan against the Six Nations, 1779*.

Canada.[45] Jemison's brother Kau-jises-tau-ge-au (Black Coals) was among them.

During the war the state of New York had eyed the western lands. After the war it first contested Massachusetts's earlier royal charter claims as well as claims from Pennsylvania and Connecticut. Beating out those states, it went on to assert its claim to Iroquois lands for the purpose of sale and development.[46]

While New York proceeded with its agenda, peace was forged between Britain and the United States in Paris on September 3, 1783. The Iroquois objected that they had not been party to the peace and were under no obligation to accept its outcome; they viewed themselves as sovereign powers. The new government disagreed. In the fall of 1784 the Continental Congress sent three commissioners to meet with both the four formerly hostile nations and the two friendly Iroquois nations at Fort Stanwix. In meetings that lasted three weeks, the United States government refused to accept the independent status of the Senecas, Cayugas, Onondagas, and Mohawks, and claimed them not "free and independent" but rather "a subdued people." The commissioners themselves reported that, "although motives of policy as well as clemency ought to incline Congress to listen to the prayers of the hostile Indians for peace," the committee suggested that the new government was "pledged to grant portions of the uncultivated lands as a bounty to their army, and in reward of their courage and fidelity . . . to make speedy provision for extending the settlement of the territories of the United States." They also suggested that such a policy would aid in dissolving the public debt through land sales.[47]

45. Abler and Tooker, "Seneca," in Trigger, ed., *Northeast*, 484. For the origins and ongoing history of that community see Sally M. Weaver, "Six Nations of the Grand River, Ontario," in Trigger, ed., *Northeast*, 525–36.

46. Jack Campisi, "The Oneida Treaty Period, 1783–1838," in Campisi and Hauptman, *The Oneida Indian Experience*, 49. Abler and Tooker, "Seneca," in Trigger, ed., *Northeast*, 508.

47. The Oneidas and the Tuscaroras, who had backed the rebel forces, were first recognized by the commissioners of the Continental Congress as "Brothers" whose "fidelity and attachment" would not be forgotten by the new government. However, by 1838 over five million acres of Oneida lands had been eaten away by threats, pressures to sell, fraud, direct payments, and offers of western land which eventually resulted in the emigration of some Oneidas to Green Bay, Wisconsin,

Anthony F. C. Wallace has labeled the years between the end of the French and Indian Wars and the close of the eighteenth century the years of "Iroquois Catastrophe." While the Oneidas lost land slowly, the diplomacy at Fort Stanwix "subjected Iroquois to physical abuse" and forced them to become signatories to treaties that separated them from their wider western claims and divided tribe from tribe, forcing negotiations on an individual rather than a confederacy basis. In the Treaty of Big Tree (1797), the Senecas sold all land west of the Genesee for $100,000 and kept reservations ranging in size from 129 square miles, at Buffalo Creek, to small reserves one and two miles square. Promises of federal and missionary assistance were thrown into the bargain. Land speculators and land-hungry settlers, some of them former members of Sullivan's invading army, came to pick up the pieces. By 1800 individual land claims (one of which was Mary Jemison's) and eleven reservations were all that was left in the United States of the former Iroquois League.[48]

In the aftermath of the breaking up of an ancient culture, the Iroquois lost their spirit and sense of purpose. White ways encroached, and as Jemison notes, none was more devastating than the use of alcohol. Hardly an abstract enemy, drink infected the Indian community, especially the menfolk, who, unlike the women, were expected to transform themselves from hunters and warriors into farmers virtually overnight.[49]

---

beginning in 1823. Campisi, "The Oneida Treaty Period," 57 and 55; Jack Campisi, "Oneida," in Trigger, ed., *Northeast*, 484–87; Seaver, *Life of Mary Jemison* (1925), pp. 92–93; Wallace, *Death and Rebirth*, 188 and chap. 7. On the impact of the Revolution on Indians see Francis Jennings, "The Indian's Revolution," in *The American Revolution in the History of American Radicalism*, ed. Alfred F. Young, (DeKalb, 1976), pp. 319–348; and Graymont, *The Iroquois and the American Revolution*, pp. 292–96.

48. Anthony F. C. Wallace, "Origins of the Longhouse Religion," in Trigger, ed., *Northeast*, 442–43; William A. Hunter, "History of the Ohio Valley," in Trigger, ed., *Northeast*, 593. On land sales as part of the Phelps and Gorham land purchase, see Abler and Tooker, "Seneca," in Trigger, ed., *Northeast*, 508–9.

49. Mary E. Young traces a similar dilemma among southern Indians in "Women, Civilization, and the Indian Question," in *Women's America*, ed. Linda K. Kerber and Jane De Hart Mathews, 149–55. Some Iroquois wished to have white help and wanted to acculturate, but others opposed American attempts at change. Divisions and often violence were the outcome of these conflicts. Wallace, *Death and Rebirth*, 202–8.

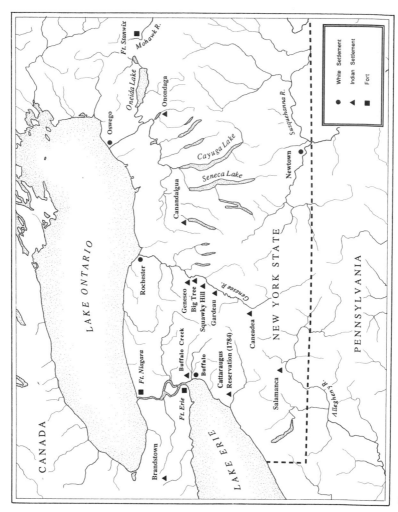

Seneca country and New York state; 1784-1824

In 1811, Jemison's eldest son, Thomas, then fifty-two, was murdered by his younger stepbrother John in a drunken fight. A year later, John (then forty-nine) killed his younger brother Jesse in another brawl. Although their mother's whiteness was able to win them some respite on their own land, as Indians they were prey to the cultural dissolution common in the postwar years.

Mary Jemison became a Seneca and lived with the Senecas until war, starvation, and the breakup of Seneca lands forced her and her family to accept the privileges they could get from living near the white world. These included eligibility for a land grant of 17,927 acres on the Gardow (Gardeau) Flats, a rich, half-mile-wide area on the left bank of the Genesee River. There the family built log cabins, farmed, raised cattle, and leased their land to tenants. At Big Tree in 1797 the land was formally granted to Jemison in a negotiation between the Senecas and the state of New York. In 1817, New York state granted her citizenship. She and her daughters continued to live on the land until various frauds, land sales, and her own old age, convinced her and her daughters to sell the remaining plots and move to the Senecas' Buffalo Creek Reservation near Buffalo.[50] She died there in 1833.

THE HISTORY OF THE BOOK AND THE CREATION OF A LEGEND

The appeal of Jemison's narrative in Seaver's presentation gave it a history in print of over 150 years. Of the first twenty editions, one was published every four and a half years between 1824 and the early twentieth century. Editors used the work in a variety of ways: as a story of bravery, a work of sentiment, a morality play, propaganda against Indian barbarity and in support of U.S. expansion, an ethnography, a tribute to white western settlers, and a children's story.

To understand why such a work had such instant popularity *and* longevity we should take note of the period in which it was published. The half century from 1824 to 1877 (the

50. Here Vail cites Lewis H. Morgan's translation of Ga-da'-o as "bank in front" (Seaver, *Life of Mary Jemison* [1925], 406); Trelease, "Mary Jemison," 271–73; Dobson, "Mary Jemison," 30. For the survival and reshaping of Seneca culture in these years, see Wallace, *Death and Rebirth*.

years of the first fourteen editions) were years of tremendous growth and change on the American continent. With the expansion from the Atlantic to the Pacific, the Civil War, rapid industrialization, immigration, and the transition of the republic from an agrarian to an urban society, the American landscape and social fabric were greatly altered. James Seaver's first edition sold over 100,000 copies in 1824. The next two imprints in England were copies of Seaver's original. Seaver's book came out the year after James Fenimore Cooper's *The Pioneers* and two years before *The Last of the Mohicans*. Both frontier authors shared best-seller status in the 1820s. Lydia Maria Child's popular historical novel *Hobomok*, the story of a Puritan woman who married an Indian, was also published in 1824. The frontier past was a recent memory to the generation of the early republic. All three books fit the emerging ideology that a once romantic and noble Indian life was becoming extinct.[51]

It is hard to prove why anyone, male or female, buys a book; nor do we have any statistics concerning who bought Jemison's editions. It can be assumed, however, that in such a climate of migration and transition, the amazing story of this small but powerful woman who lived ninety years at a critical time in the nation's history would be of special interest to female readers. Women of all classes and backgrounds were touched by those national changes, as were their tastes, their levels of education, and their literacy. By the Revolutionary period, most white women in the country could read.[52] Education was far from universal, but in the Northeast academies and seminaries were open for many young women, even those of relatively modest means. In the antebellum years changes in book and magazine production occurred

51. Frank Luther Mott, *Golden Multitudes: The Story of Best Sellers in the United States*, 304–6; Lydia Maria Child, *Hobomok and Other Writings of Indians*, ed. Carolyn L. Karcher, xvii. Pearce calls this belief in the inevitable conquest by "civilization" of the "noble"-but-soon-to-become-extinct savage "a melancholy fact" commonly believed between 1777 and 1851 (*Savagism and Civilization*, 53–75).

52. Margaret Spufford, "First Steps in Literacy: The Reading and Writing Experience of the Humblest Seventeenth-Century Spiritual Autobiographer," in Harvey J. Graff, ed., *Literacy and Social Development in the West*, 125–50, and E. Jennifer Monaghan, "Literacy Instruction and Gender in Colonial New England," *American Quarterly* 40 (March, 1988): 18–41.

simultaneously with a rise in the number of middle-class women readers, creating a new female demand in the literary marketplace and a place for women writers to fill that demand.[53]

The Seaver offering was also an example of another popular nineteenth-century literary form—the as-told-to life stories of Native Americans. Dozens of such narratives have come to us filtered and transformed by their white editors and amanuenses. These books catered to the nineteenth-century fascination with the "other" by offering pictures of Indian life. Seaver's book offered that attraction along with the story of a white woman on the earlier frontier.[54]

Of course Seaver and his book's subsequent editors had their own notions of Indian life and American history. These were imposed on the editions in a variety of ways. Seaver was the first of many editors to add treatises on Indian religion, government, courtship, family, death, and supposed "credulity." He, less intrusively than some who followed him, found it necessary to include accounts asserting justice on the American side in the face of Indian "barbarities." In several later editions such justifications were added to Jemison's account as if *she* had said them. Other additions were added in a thirty-eight-page appendix. Seaver's 1824 appendix occasionally gives her as a source of information, though frequently no source is provided. Because of these problems, all editions of the book, but especially those published *after* 1824, should be used with care.[55]

53. Nina Baym, *Novels, Readers, and Reviewers*; Janice A. Radway, *Reading the Romance*, 3–45 and 186–222; Jane Tompkins, *Sensational Designs* (New York, 1985), xi–xix and 122–85.

54. Gretchen M. Bataille and Kathleen Mullen Sands, *American Indian Women*.

55. Seaver includes a full description of the celebration of the last moon at the end of January, but after giving these details from Jemison, tells us that the meal is a "mess" that is devoured without much ceremony." Seaver *Life of Mary Jemison* (1925), app., 164–67. "Of the Manner of Farming, as Practiced by the Indian Women" is one section from Seaver's appendix often attributed to Jemison, but Seaver never tells us this is the case. It says "all work together in one field, or at whatever job they may have on hand. In the spring they choose an old active squaw to be their driver and overseer when at labor, for the ensuing year. She accepts the honor, and they consider themselves bound to obey her." During the planting women meet together in the morning, and once in the field they work together, row by row, until "the whole is finished. By this rule they perform their labor of every kind, and every jealousy of one having done more or less than another, is effectively

Besides making additions, Seaver either left out or perhaps did not ask questions about many aspects of Seneca life, especially a Seneca woman's life. The narrative itself has little from Jemison on the role of Seneca ceremonies and religion, the mythic thought world of the Senecas, their music and dance, the wealth of things that they produced from their own traditions, and their adaptations of the new materials brought by European contact. Again, material in the appendix is randomly added and never clearly attributed to particular authors. These are significant omissions, especially for our understanding of Jemison as she became a Seneca woman. Without such information, we can only speculate about the spiritual and material power of the Seneca world.

Jemison's second husband, Hiokatoo (pronounced Hi-o-ga'too or Hi-gi-doa), was her spouse for nearly fifty years and the father of six of her children, but she said hardly anything about him to Seaver. Chapter 11 with its biography of Hiokatoo was created completely by Seaver from the words of a man who called himself George Jemison and claimed kinship with Mary. In his Introduction, Seaver explained that, "For the life of her last husband, we are indebted to her cousin, Mr. George Jemison, to whom she referred us for information on that subject generally. The thoughts of his deeds, probably chilled her old heart, and made her dread to rehearse them," but "she had frequently heard" them, according to the doctor. Midway through the chapter Seaver's footnote reminds the reader that the material is from George Jemison. Seaver testifies to its accuracy, despite Mrs. Jemison's recounting to him how the alleged George Jemison had cheated her out of her land, and her belief that he was no relation to her whatever. In the 1840 edition Hiokatoo's "fierce warrior" image was augmented with a bizarre woodcut titled "Hiokatoo, Mrs. Jemison's second husband, as he appeared when attired in his war dress." A strange, dark figure indeed, Hiokatoo stands at the ready, a rifle over his shoulder and a knife in hand. A nineteenth-century reader might wonder what the "white woman" would do with such a fearsome creature. Such sup-

avoided." Seaver, *Life of Mary Jemison* (1925), app., 175–76. Similar accounts are found in Father Joseph François Lafitau, *Customs of the American Indians Compared with the Customs of Primitive Tribes*, ed. and trans. William N. Fenton and Elizabeth L. Moore, 2, 54–55.

posedly biographical notes and drawings tell us more about
the editor's need to perpetuate notions of the barbarity of
Indian men and Revolutionary American purity than they
tell us about Hiokatoo.[56]

Another problem with Seaver's narrative is its language.
Clearly a product of his class and his age, Seaver frequently
modified Jemison's words to conform to a sentimental style
popular in his day. The published account can hardly have
been taken from her word for word. The usage is often flow-
ery, and the sensibility and vocabulary more that of a middle-
class woman from Philadelphia than a frontier woman unable
to read English, who lived most of her life speaking Seneca.[57]
An early edition's title assures us that the work was "Carefully
Taken from Her Own Words by James E. Seaver." The
emphasis justifiably should be on "taken from," but the question arises, What happened to her words? It is difficult for the
reader to know which were really Jemison's own words, and
which were doctored up by the good doctor. Straightforward
speech is probably the best indicator of Jemison's language.[58]

When James Seaver became ill and died in 1827, his
brother William took up the Jemison legacy. Claiming that
under the pressures of preparing the first edition his brother's
ill health "tended greatly to disqualify him for mental or
physical exertion" and contributed to its "defects," the new
editor expressed the need for changes. William argued for
those revisions that would make the work into "what the
author originally intended it should be; a faithful, interesting

56. Hiokatoo's name is also spelled Hiadagoo The pronunciation suggested
was from Myrtle Peterson. William N. Fenton broke down the name's meaning into
the components "he"/"spear point"/"large," and suggested the linguistic pronunciation Hagido:wa (correspondence, December 5, 1988). For Seaver on George Jemison, see his Introduction, p. 58 below. Jemison's account of George Jemison may
be found in chaps. 13 and 14. For other views see Barbara Graymont, *Iroquois in
the American Revolution*, 168–174, and Wallace, who analyzes the role of the warrior
in Seneca society in *Death and Rebirth*, 135–38.

57. See Allen W. Trelease's similar remarks on the narrative's language in his
Introduction to James E. Seaver, *A Narrative of the Life of Mrs. Mary Jemison* (1824
rpr., Gloucester, 1975).

58. James E. Seaver, *Deh-he-wa-mis; or A Narrative of the Life of Mary Jemison:
Otherwise Called the White Woman, Who Was Taken Captive by the Indians in MDCCLV;
and Who Continued with Them Seventy-Eight Years, Containing an Account of the
Murder of Her Father and His Family, Her Marriages and Sufferings, Indian Barbarities, Customs and Traditions. Carefully Taken from Her Own Words by James E. Seaver*,
2d ed. (Batavia, N.Y., 1842).

and instructive history, of the subject and events to which it relates."[59] In 1842, William Seaver and Son brought in Ebenezer Mix, a land speculator and lawyer in the Genesee valley, to help make such "improvements."

Under the new management, the edition of 1842 began the relentless process of whitewashing Mrs. Jemison by highlighting the contrast between a white woman's culture and a "savage" unchristian world. The words "white woman" first appear in the title together in bold type with Jemison's supposed Seneca name: *DEH-HE-WÄ-MIS or A Narrative of the Life of Mary Jemison: Otherwise Called THE WHITE WOMAN.* . . . The new introduction tells readers that they will clearly understand the need for perpetuating the gospel among the heathen after reading the narrative. It is in the second edition that we find the first public statement of Jemison's alleged deathbed conversion to Christianity, claimed by Mrs. Laura Wright and her husband, Rev. Asher Wright, who was a missionary to the Seneca.[60]

Mix added three chapters and four articles to James Seaver's original. Most striking to the modern reader are the three chapters that were inserted in the text as if they had been part of Jemison's narrative, including the alleged progress in central and western New York since the departure of its former native residents. In a final attempt to turn Jemison's work into a justification for taking over New York, a chapter on General Sullivan's expedition was added. Strongly defending the invasion of Iroquois territory during the Revolution, it stands in sharp contrast to Jemison's description of the

59. James Seaver, *Deh-he-wa-mis; or A Narrative of the Life of Mary Jemison: Otherwise Called the White Woman, Who Was Taken Captive by the Indians in MDCCLV; and Who Continued with them Seventy-eight Years. Carefully Taken from Her Own Words* . . . (Devon and London, 1847), iii. This statement is also is found in the 1842 or sixth Utica edition.

60. Seaver, *De-he-wä-mis: or A Narrative of the Life of Mary Jemison: Otherwise Called the White Woman, Who Was Taken Captive by the Indians in MDCCLV: and Who Continued with Them Seventy Eight Years* . . . (Batavia, N.Y., 1842X; Devon and London, 1847), vii. On the "conversion" see Namias, "White Captives," 326–28, and Vail's comments in Seaver, *Life of Mary Jemison* (1925), 430. Vail counts the William Seaver and Son editions as the second "old" edition, but lists seven other variations and abridgements in England and America as "new" editions. I regard his "old" editions as "editions" since these are the major revisions. See the "Tabulation of Editions of *The Life of Mary Jemison*" in Vail, *Life of Mary Jemison* (1925), 296–97.

devastation wreaked on the Senecas by Revolutionary forces, of which the ultimate results were the exile of most of the Iroquois to Canada or their settlement onto reservations. William Seaver and Son printed one edition in 1842 and two in 1844—all including these Mix "improvements."[61]

In 1856, Lewis Henry Morgan, anthropologist and student of Iroquoia, helped edit a new Jemison edition. Although three of the preceding eleven imprints had minimal illustrations, Morgan's had five wood engravings by Charles Spiegle and Charles E. Johnson, one a frontispiece and the others facing the opening pages of four chapters. The somewhat fanciful, romantic drawings and the brutal and violent drawing, *The Murder of One of Her Sons, by His Brother*, indicate the both romantic and Indian-hating audience to which this new edition was to appeal. Morgan Indianized his edition as well. He added as an appendix a list of Iroquois place-names; notes augmenting, verifying, or contradicting Jemison's and Seaver's discussions of Iroquois life; and sections of his work *The League of the Iroquois* (1851). A letter from Seneca sachem Ely S. Parker (Don-ne-ho-ga'-weh) testifies that the Jemison story is "entirely true" and related closely to "the traditional history preserved of her among the Indians with whom she lived and died." The illustrations, the larger print, and the extensive notes (including all of Mix's additions and Morgan's own) increased the length by an additional 120 pages, for a total of 312 pages. Three printings were published between 1856 and 1860.[62]

In 1877 ironworks magnate William Pryor Letchworth became yet another shaper of Jemison's legacy. His interest in a wide variety of benevolent works and his buying up of huge tracts of Genesee land brought him in contact with local Indian lore and Mary Jemison in particular. Like many white Americans of his time, Letchworth believed that Indians would soon become extinct. On his one thousand acres, he

61. Mix's chapters are 5, 7, and 15 in Seaver, *Life of Mary Jemison* (1856) and Seaver, *Deh-he-wa-mis* (1844), 173 and 177–78. These were William Seaver and Son editions. See Vail's notes in *Life of Mary Jemison* (1925), 288, 292–93.

62. In Seaver, *Life of Mary Jemison* (1856), where Parker's letter follows the table of contents. James E. Seaver, *A Narrative of the Life of Mary Jemison: The White Woman of the Genesee*, rev. ed. by Charles Delamater Vail (New York, 1918), 292, and Seaver, *Life of Mary Jemison* (1925), 296–97. Rochester printer D. M. Dewey produced the first 1856 edition.

LIFE

OF

MARY JEMISON:

DEH-HE-WÄ-MIS.

By JAMES E. SEAVER.

FOURTH EDITION,

WITH GEOGRAPHICAL AND EXPLANATORY NOTES

NEW YORK AND AUBURN:
MILLER, ORTON & MULLIGAN.
ROCHESTER: D. M. DEWEY.
1856.

RELATING HER HISTORY TO THE AUTHOR.

1856 frontispiece and title page. Courtesy of the Rare Books and Special Collections, Rush Rhees Library, University of Rochester.

studied the Iroquois and became interested in preserving traces of earlier Indian life. His fascination with Mary Jemison is reflected in his private papers by an extensive correspondence with others about her life. Letchworth's new editions visually supplemented the Jemison narrative with between seventeen and twenty-two illustrations, including many taken from Morgan's *The League of the Iroquois*, showing Seneca dress, moccasins, cradleboards, and adornments. Between 1877 and 1913, Letchworth published three different revisions for a total of five editions. The last three printings were issued in New York and London by G. P. Putnam's Sons.

Letchworth's interest in Jemison did not stop with Seaver's narrative. He saw Jemison as a romantic figure, a white Indian of the woods, connecting Americans of the Victorian age with the sacrifices of early frontier settlement. He had her bones moved from her burial place at the Seneca Mission House in Buffalo to a special plot of ground near her old home on what was then his land on the Genesee River south of Rochester, near Castile, New York.[63] Before his death he left this estate (including Jemison's burial plot) to the state of New York for the establishment of a park. Two years before he died, Letchworth commissioned Henry K. Bush-Brown to build a bronze sculpture memorializing Jemison's life. He also purchased and moved her daughter Nancy's house from the lower Genesee to face the statue on higher ground, setting it beside another purchase, an early Seneca meetinghouse. All of these stand today in Letchworth State Park, as does the William Prior Letchworth Museum, complete with Jemison pictures, dedications, and other tributes.[64]

Around the time Letchworth died, and shortly after, the Jemison legacy was continued by Charles Delamater Vail. A New York bibliophile and member of the New York Scenic

63. Seaver, *Life of Mary Jemison* (1925), 292–93. Karen Haltunnin, *Confidence Men and Painted Women*, chap. 5.

64. Letters to and from Bush-Brown may be found in the Milne Library, State University College of Arts and Sciences at Geneseo, N.Y., in the William Prior Letchworth Collection. For a fuller discussion of this relationship and its meaning to the Jemison legend, see June Namias, "White Captives," chap. 6, and June Namias, *White Captives: Gender and Ethnicity on Successive American Frontiers* (forthcoming), chap. 5. Sixty-three editions are listed by Vail in his "Tabulation of Editions of *The Life of Mary Jemison*" in Seaver, *Life of Mary Jemison* (1925), 293.

and Historic Preservation Society, Vail did extensive research into the history of the various Jemison editions housed in rare book collections around the country. He also took up the task of continuing research into Jemison's white and Indian pasts. Very much the gentleman historian and antiquarian, Vail had his New York society produce the largest, most profusely illustrated, and heavily annotated edition of the Jemison narrative ever published. His 1918 and 1925 editions number 475 and 483 pages respectively and have forty-one illustrations. A gold-leaf illustration shows Bush-Brown's statue on the forest green cover of the 1918 edition.[65]

A final figure in the history of Jemison's popularity is Lois Lenski, a popular writer of juvenile fiction in the 1930s and 1970s. Lenski wrote and illustrated nearly one hundred internationally known children's books, including *Indian Captive: The Story of Mary Jemison*. She took over three years to research *Indian Captive*. With twenty printings in the United States and abroad, *Indian Captive* sold approximately 90,000 copies in hard cover. In 1941, the first year it was issued, the book won a Newbery Honor Book award for distinction among childrens' books. It went into fifteen printings. Lenski's pert, inquisitive, and feeling Jemison, more a nine-year-old than an adolescent, offers a generally sympathetic view of Seneca life and of Jemison's choice of becoming Indian. Although the little blonde heroine upstages the Indians and never does get tan despite her hours of picking corn, Lenski's appreciation of the Seneca world certainly contrasts with the "improvements" of Mix a hundred years earlier.[66]

Surveying the versions of the Jemison story, we notice that although several revisers introduced Jemison's narrative as a fall from civilization into barbarism, her life offered readers a heroic frontier model as well. Unlike many of her male counterparts in the move west, she did not shoot Indians

65. Seaver, *Life of Mary Jemison* (1918). This edition was revised again in 1925 and 1929. "Tabulation" in Strecker, *My First Years as a Jemisonian*.
66. Taimi M. Ranta, "Lois Lenski," 241–52; Clare D. Kinsman, "Lois Lenski," *Contemporary Authors: A Bio-Bibliographical Guide to Current Authors*, vol. 1 (Detroit, 1975), pp. 372–73; Lenski, *Indian Captive*. Other children's authors beside Lenski have written books on Jemison. For all editions, consult Library of Congress listings. Publisher J. B. Lippincott kept reissuing *Indian Captive* until 1969. Publication figures from correspondence, Laura Godwin, J. B. Lippincott, Harper and Row Junior Books, July 19, 1988.

or try to "tame" the wilderness; she was, however, a figure of stature. Certainly Seaver saw this from the start. Jemison had walked hundreds of miles, and had lived through family loss and the displacements of war and revolution. Her story appealed as well to the interest in the exotic. The early illustrations of strange and "wild" Indians, and later children's book drawings of Mary picking corn and playing among the Senecas, brought readers an exciting and foreign world. There they may have identified with the story's heroine and wondered whether they would have faired as well in her place. Such a combination that simultaneously asks us to put ourselves in the place of the heroine and makes us admire her endurance was the kind of uplifting story heartily devoured by nineteenth-century readers.

The Continuing Jemison Legacy

Mary Jemison's life is the story of a white captive, a woman who is a survivor, a woman able to mediate between cultures. Her generosity and lack of rancor, her acute eye and her physical strength despite her small frame, her psychic ability to endure loss and continue to lead a productive life, and finally, her generativity, make her something of a heroine with whom a contemporary reader can identify.

There is one last word to be said. Mary Jemison is not just a figure of history, dead, buried, and reburied, with a statue over her. Iroquois people still know her, often by her name, Degiwene's (pronounced De-kee-wa'nis), meaning "two falling voices" or "two-voices-falling." She has a great many living descendants, especially in western New York and in southern Canada. To these descendants and to Iroquois people, she is a very real figure affirming the possibility that whites and Indians might have lived together peacefully, and an example of those things that went wrong. For G. Peter Jemison, a descendant and a contemporary Seneca artist, Mary tells the Senecas' side of the Revolution. She was fluent in two languages. Her story is important because while Indian life is typically rendered as brutal and wretched, Jemison demonstrates the "kindness she was shown" and the "stature" in which she was held by Seneca people. She also depicts how a white woman who became an Indian was "swindled out of her land by her own people," who deceived her and took advantage of her old age. Finally, though "her life was difficult," and there were things with which she disagreed, "she chose to stay."[67]

To Wanda Overhiser, descended from Mary on her father's side, studying Jemison's life gives a sense of belonging and accomplishment, and a sense of family tradition. "She's my grandmother, how many down the way." To her, Jemison represents "the stamina of the human spirit—five generations down." She and other ancestors "didn't break down, didn't fall apart. . . . They kept right on going."[68]

NOTE ON THIS EDITION

The present edition follows the earlier ones by making Seaver's narrative its core. I have chosen to go back to the original 1824 edition because each subsequent one became more and more encumbered with editors' notes. Here Seaver's original spelling and grammar are intact with the exception of occasional typographical errors in the text. I have omitted Seaver's original appendix. This may distress some readers who are familiar with the earlier editions, but my critique of the appendix above should explain the reasoning behind the decision. The aim of this edition is to recover Mary Jemison's own words as fully as possible. Although this is an elusive task, it would be even more so with the additions from later editions that attempted to remake Jemison into a white Christian martyr among the savages and to justify United States Indian policy.[69]

As problematic as James E. Seaver's work is as a representation of the actual life of Jemison, it is closer to the source than later ones. Local New Yorkers called on him to interview Jemison; he spoke with her, and he made the original decisions how to edit her story. His closeness to his subject gave him a better sense of her meaning and emphasis than later revisers, no matter how dedicated. Although Seaver's rendi-

67. Jemison's Seneca name and pronunciation from Myrtle Peterson, with translation and alternative pronunciation as De-gi-wa-nis from William Fenton. Telephone conversation with G. Peter Jemison, from Victor, N.Y., August 14, 1986.
68. Telephone conversation with Wanda Overhiser in Rochester, N.Y., May 8, 1987.
69. For a fuller discussion of all the additions to Seaver's text and more analysis of their meanings see Namias, *White Captives* (forthcoming), chap. 5.

tion is not pure, it is the best we have. If we still cannot know completely which passages are Seaver's and which are Jemison's, we at least do not have to contend with others who, whatever merits their works possessed, obfuscated Mary Jemison's life more than they clarified it.

A NARRATIVE OF THE
LIFE OF MRS. MARY JEMISON

AUTHOR'S
PREFACE

THAT to biographical writings we are indebted for the greatest and best field in which to study mankind, or human nature, is a fact duly appreciated by a well-informed community. In them we can trace the effects of mental operations to their proper sources; and by comparing our own composition with that of those who have excelled in virtue, or with that of those who have been sunk in the lowest depths of folly and vice, we are enabled to select a plan of life that will at least afford self-satisfaction, and guide us through the world in paths of morality.

Without a knowledge of the lives of the vile and abandoned, we should be wholly incompetent to set an appropriate value upon the charms, the excellence and the worth of those principles which have produced the finest traits in the characters of the most virtuous.

Biography is a telescope of life, through which we can see the extremes and excesses of the varied properties of the human heart. Wisdom and folly, refinement and vulgarity, love and hatred, tenderness and cruelty, happiness and misery, piety and infidelity, commingled with every other cardinal virtue or vice, are to be seen on the variegated pages of the history of human events, and are eminently deserving the attention of those who would learn to walk in the "paths of peace."

The brazen statue and the sculptured marble, can commemorate the greatness of heroes, statesmen, philosophers, and blood-stained conquerors, who have risen to the zenith of human glory and popularity, under the influence of the mild sun of prosperity: but it is the faithful page of biography that transmits to future generations the poverty, pain, wrong, hunger, wretchedness and torment, and every nameless misery that has been endured by those who have lived in obscurity, and groped their lonely way through a long series of unpropitious events, with but little help besides the light of nature. While the gilded monument displays in brightest colors the vanity of pomp, and the emptiness of nominal greatness, the biographical page, that lives in every line, is giving lessons of fortitude in time of danger, patience in suffering, hope in distress, invention in necessity, and resignation to unavoidable evils. Here also may be learned, pity for the bereaved, benevolence for the destitute, and compassion for the helpless; and at the same time all the sympathies of the soul will be naturally excited to sigh at the unfavorable result, or to smile at the fortunate relief.

In the great inexplicable chain which forms the circle of human events, each individual link is placed on a level with the others, and performs an equal task; but, as the world is partial, it is the situation that attracts the attention of mankind, and excites the unfortunate vociferous eclat of elevation, that raises the pampered parasite to such an immense height in the scale of personal vanity, as, generally, to deprive him of respect, before he can return to a state of equilibrium with his fellows, or to the place whence he started.

Few great men have passed from the stage of action, who have not left in the history of their lives indelible marks of ambition or folly, which produced insurmountable reverses, and rendered the whole a mere caricature, that can be examined only with disgust and regret. Such pictures, however, are profitable, for "by others' faults wise men correct their own."

The following is a piece of biography, that shows what changes may be affected in the animal and mental constitution of man; what trials may be surmounted; what cruelties perpetrated, and what pain endured, when stern necessity holds the reins, and drives the car of fate.

As books of this kind are sought and read with avidity, especially by children, and are well calculated to excite their attention, inform their understanding, and improve them in the art of reading, the greatest care has been observed to render the style easy, the language comprehensive, and the description natural. Prolixity has been studiously avoided. The line of distinction between virtue and vice has been rendered distinctly visible; and chastity of expression and sentiment have received due attention. Strict fidelity has been observed in the composition: consequently, no circumstance has been intentionally exaggerated by the paintings of fancy, nor by fine flashes of rhetoric: neither has the picture been rendered more dull than the original. Without the aid of fiction, what was received as matter of fact, only has been recorded.

It will be observed that the subject of this narrative has arrived at least to the advanced age of eighty years; that she is destitute of education; and that her journey of life, throughout its texture, has been interwoven with troubles, which ordinarily are calculated to impair the faculties of the mind; and it will be remembered, that there are but few old people who can recollect with precision the circumstances of their lives, (particularly those circumstances which transpired after middle age.) If, therefore, any error shall be discovered in the narration in respect to time, it will be overlooked by the kind reader, or charitably placed to the narrator's account, and not imputed to neglect, or to the want of attention in the compiler.

The appendix is principally taken from the words of Mrs. Jemison's statements. Those parts which were not derived from her, are deserving equal credit, having been obtained from authentic sources.*

For the accommodation of the reader, the work has been divided into chapters, and a copious table of contents affixed. The introduction will facilitate the understanding of what follows; and as it contains matter that could not be inserted with propriety in any other place, will be read with interest and satisfaction.

Having finished my undertaking, the subsequent pages are cheerfully submitted to the perusal and approbation or animadversion of a candid, generous and indulgent public.

* The appendix has been omitted from this edition. See Editor's Introduction, p. 44 above.

At the same time it is fondly hoped that the lessons of distress that are pourtrayed, may have a direct tendency to increase our love of liberty; to enlarge our views of the blessings that are derived from our liberal institutions; and to excite in our breasts sentiments of devotion and gratitude to the great Author and finisher of our happiness.

Pembroke, March 1, 1824

AUTHOR'S
INTRODUCTION

THE Peace of 1783, and the consequent cessation of Indian hostilities and barbarities, returned to their friends those prisoners, who had escaped the tomahawk, the gauntlet, and the savage fire, after their having spent many years in captivity, and restored harmony to society.

The stories of Indian cruelties which were common in the new settlements, and were calamitous realities previous to that propitious event; slumbered in the minds that had been constantly agitated by them, and were only roused occasionally, to become the fearful topic of the fireside.

It is presumed that at this time there are but few native Americans that have arrived to middle age, who cannot distinctly recollect of sitting in the chimney corner when children, all contracted with fear, and there listening to their parents or visitors, while they related stories of Indian conquests, and murders, that would make their flaxen hair nearly stand erect, and almost destroy the power of motion.

At the close of the Revolutionary war; all that part of the State of New-York that lies west of Utica was uninhabited by white people, and few indeed had ever passed beyond Fort Stanwix, except when engaged in war against the Indians, who were numerous, and occupied a number of large towns between the Mohawk river and lake Erie. Sometime elapsed after this event, before the country about the lakes and on the Genesee river was visited, save by an occasional land speculator, or by defaulters who wished by retreating to what in those days was deemed almost the end of the earth, to escape the force of civil law.

At length, the richness and fertility of the soil excited emigration, and here and there a family settled down and commenced improvements in the country which had recently been the property of the aborigines. Those who settled near the Genesee river, soon became acquainted with "The White Woman," as Mrs. Jemison is called, whose history they anxiously sought, both as a matter of interest and curiosity. Frankness characterized her conduct, and without reserve she would readily gratify them by relating some of the most important periods of her life.

Although her bosom companion was an ancient Indian warrior, and notwithstanding her children and associates were all Indians, yet it was found that she possessed an uncommon share of hospitality, and that her friendship was well worth courting and preserving. Her house was the stranger's home; from her table the hungry were refreshed;—she made the naked as comfortable as her means would admit of; and in all her actions, discovered so much natural goodness of heart, that her admirers increased in proportion to the extension of her acquaintance, and she became celebrated as the friend of the distressed. She was the protectress of the homeless fugitive, and made welcome the weary wanderer. Many still live to commemorate her benevolence towards them, when prisoners during the war, and to ascribe their deliverance to the mediation of "The White Woman."

The settlements increased, and the whole country around her was inhabited by a rich and respectable people, principally from New-England, as much distinguished for their spirit of inquisitiveness as for their habits of industry and honesty, who had all heard from one source and another a part of her life in detached pieces, and had obtained an idea that the whole taken in connection would afford instruction and amusement.

Many gentlemen of respectability, felt anxious that her narrative might be laid before the public, with a view not only to perpetuate the remembrance of the atrocities of the savages in former times, but to preserve some historical facts which they supposed to be intimately connected with her life, and which otherwise must be lost.

Forty years had passed since the close of the Revolutionary war, and almost seventy years had seen Mrs. Jemison with the Indians, when Daniel W. Banister, Esq. at the instance of several gentlemen, and prompted by his own ambition to add something to the accumulating fund of useful knowledge, resolved, in the autumn of 1823, to embrace that time, while she was capable of recollecting and reciting the scenes through which she had passed, to collect from herself, and to publish to the world, an accurate account of her life.

I was employed to collect the materials, and prepare the work for the press; and accordingly went to the house of Mrs. Jennet Whaley in the town of Castile, Genesee co. N.Y. in company with the publisher, who procured the interesting subject of the following narrative, to come to that place (a distance of four miles) and there repeat the story of her eventful life. She came on foot in company with Mr. Thomas Clute, whom she considers her protector, and tarried almost three days, which time was busily occupied in taking a sketch of her narrative as she recited it.

Her appearance was well calculated to excite a great degree of sympathy in a stranger, who had been partially informed of her origin, when comparing her present situation with what it probably would have been, had she been permitted to have remained with her friends, and to have enjoyed the blessings of civilization.

In stature she is very short, and considerably under the middle size, and stands tolerably erect, with her head bent forward, apparently from her having for a long time been accustomed to carrying heavy burdens in a strap placed across her forehead. Her complexion is very white for a woman of her age, and although the wrinkles of fourscore years are deeply indented in her cheeks, yet the crimson of youth is distinctly visible. Her eyes are light blue, a little faded by age, and naturally brilliant and sparkling. Her sight is quite dim, though she is able to perform her necessary labor without the assistance of glasses. Her cheek bones are high, and rather prominent, and her front teeth, in the lower jaw, are sound and good. When she looks up and is engaged in conversation her countenance is very expressive; but from her long residence with the Indians, she has acquired the habit of peeping from under eye brows as they do with the head inclined downwards. Formerly her hair was of a light chesnut brown— it is now quite grey, a little curled, of middling length and tied in a bunch behind. She informed me that she had never worn a cap nor a comb.

She speaks English plainly and distinctly, with a little of the Irish emphasis, and has the use of words so well as to render herself intelligible on any subject with which she is acquainted. Her recollection and memory exceeded my expectation. It cannot be reasonably supposed, that a person of her age has kept the events of seventy years in so complete a chain as to be able to assign to each its proper time and place; she, however, made her recital with as few obvious mistakes as might be found in that of a person of fifty.

She walks with a quick step without a staff, and I was informed by Mr. Clute, that she could yet cross a stream on a log or pole as steadily as any other person.

Her passions are easily excited. At a number of periods in her narrative, tears trickled down her grief worn cheek, and at the same time a rising sigh would stop her utterance.

Industry is a virtue which she has uniformly practiced from the day of her adoption to the present. She pounds her samp, cooks for herself, gathers and chops wood, feeds her cattle and poultry, and performs other laborious services. Last season she planted, tended and gathered corn—in short, she is always busy.

Her dress at the time I saw her, was made and worn after the Indian fashion, and consisted of a shirt, short gown, petticoat, stockings, moccasins, a blanket and a bonnet. The shirt was of cotton and made at the top, as I was informed, like a man's without collar or sleeves—was open before and extended down about midway of the hips.—The petticoat was a piece of broadcloth with the list at the top and bottom and the ends sewed together. This was tied on by a string that was passed over it and around the waist, in such a manner as to let the bottom of the petticoat down half way between the knee and ankle and leave one-fourth of a yard at the top to be turned down over the string—the bottom of the shirt coming a little below, and on the outside of the top of the fold so as to leave the list and two or three inches of the cloth uncovered. The stockings, were of blue broadcloth, tied, or pinned on, which reached from the knees, into the mouth of the moccasins.—Around her toes only she had some rags, and over these her buckskin moccasins. Her gown was of undressed flannel, colored brown. It was made in old yankee style, with long sleeves, covered the top of the hips, and was tied before in two places with strings of deer skin. Over all this, she wore an Indian blanket. On her head she wore a piece of old brown woolen cloth made somewhat like a sun bonnet.

Such was the dress that this woman was contented to wear, and habit had rendered it convenient and comfortable. She wore it not as a matter of necessity, but from choice, for it will be seen in the sequel, that her property is sufficient to enable her to dress in the best fashion, and to allow her every comfort of life.

Her house, in which she lives, is 20 by 28 feet; built of square timber, with a shingled roof, and a framed stoop. In the centre of the house is a chimney of stones and sticks, in which there are two fire places. She has a good framed barn, 26 by 36, well filled, and owns a fine stock of cattle and horses. Besides the buildings above mentioned, she owns a number of houses that are occupied by tenants, who work her flats upon shares.

Her dwelling, is about one hundred rods north of the Great Slide, a curiosity that will be described in its proper place, on the west side of the Genesee river.

Mrs. Jemison, appeared sensible of her ignorance of the manners of the white people, and for that reason, was not familiar, except with those with whom she was intimately acquainted. In fact she was (to appearance) so jealous of her rights, or that she should say something that would be injurious to herself or family, that if Mr. Clute had not been present, we should have been unable to have obtained her history. She, however, soon became free and unembarrassed in her conversation, and spoke with a degree of mildness, candor and simplicity, that is calculated to remove all doubts as to the veracity of the speaker. The vices of the Indians, she appeared disposed not to aggravate, and seemed to take pride in extoling their virtues. A kind of family pride inclined her to withhold whatever would blot the character of her descendants, and perhaps induced her to keep back many things that would have been interesting.

For the life of her last husband, we are indebted to her cousin, Mr. George Jemison, to whom she referred us for information on that subject generally. The thoughts of his deeds, probably chilled her old heart, and made her dread to rehearse them, and at the same time she well knew they were no secret, for she had frequently heard him relate the whole, not only to her cousin, but to others.

Before she left us she was very sociable, and she resumed her naturally pleasant countenance, enlivened with a smile.

Her neighbors speak of her as possessing one of the happiest tempers and dispositions, and give her the name of never having done a censurable act to their knowledge.

Her habits, are those of the Indians—she sleeps on skins without a bedstead, sits upon the floor or on a bench, and holds her victuals on her lap, or in her hands.

Her ideas of religion, correspond in every respect with those of the great mass of the Senecas. She applauds virtue, and despises vice. She believes in a future state, in which the good will be happy, and the bad miserable; and that the acquisition of that happiness, depends primarily upon human volition, and the consequent good deeds of the happy recipient of blessedness. The doctrines taught in the Christian religion, she is a stranger to.

Her daughters are said to be active and enterprising women, and her grandsons, who arrived to manhood, are considered able, decent and respectable men in their tribe.

Having in this cursory manner, introduced the subject of the following pages, I proceed to the narration of a life that has been viewed with attention, for a great number of years by a few, and which will be read by the public with the mixed sensations of pleasure and pain, and with interest, anxiety and satisfaction.

A NARRATIVE OF THE
LIFE OF MRS. MARY JEMISON

1

Nativity of her Parents.—Their removal to America.—Her Birth.—Parents settle in Pennsylvania.—Omen of her Captivity.

ALTHOUGH I may have frequently heard the history of my ancestry, my recollection is too imperfect to enable me to trace it further back than to my father and mother, whom I have often heard mention the families from whence they originated, as having possessed wealth and honorable stations under the government of the country in which they resided.

On the account of the great length of time that has elapsed since I was separated from my parents and friends, and having heard the story of their nativity only in the days of my childhood, I am not able to state positively, which of the two countries, Ireland or Scotland, was the land of my parents' birth and education. It, however, is my impression, that they were born and brought up in Ireland.

My Father's name was Thomas Jemison, and my mother's, before her marriage with him, was Jane Erwin. Their affection for each other was mutual, and of that happy kind which tends directly to sweeten the cup of life; to render connubial sorrows lighter; to assuage every discontentment; and to promote not only their own comfort, but that of all who come within the circle of their acquaintance. Of their happiness I recollect to have heard them speak; and the remembrance I yet retain of their mildness and perfect agreement in the government of their children, together with their

61

mutual attention to our common education, manners, religious instruction and wants, renders it a fact in my mind, that they were ornaments to the married state, and examples of connubial love, worthy of imitation. After my remembrance, they were strict observers of religious duties; for it was the daily practice of my father, morning and evening, to attend, in his family, to the worship of God.

Resolved to leave the land of their nativity, they removed from their residence to a port in Ireland, where they lived but a short time before they set sail for this country, in the year 1742 or 3, on board the ship Mary William, bound to Philadelphia, in the state of Pennsylvania.

The intestine divisions, civil wars, and ecclesiastical rigidity and domination that prevailed in those days, were the causes of their leaving their mother country, to find a home in the American wilderness, under the mild and temperate government of the descendants of William Penn; where, without fear, they might worship God, and perform their usual avocations.

In Europe my parents had two sons and one daughter, whose names were John, Thomas and Betsey; with whom, after having put their effects on board, they embarked, leaving a large connexion of relatives and friends, under all those painful sensations, which are only felt when kindred souls give the parting hand and last farewell to those to whom they are endeared by every friendly tie.

In the course of their voyage I was born, to be the sport of fortune and almost an outcast to civil society; to stem the current of adversity through a long chain of vicissitudes, unsupported by the advice of tender parents, or the hand of an affectionate friend; and even without the enjoyment, from others, of any of those tender sympathies that are adapted to the sweetening of society, except such as naturally flow from uncultivated minds, that have been calloused by ferocity.

Excepting my birth, nothing remarkable occurred to my parents on their passage, and they were safely landed at Philadelphia. My father being fond of rural life, and having been bred to agricultural pursuits, soon left the city, and removed his family to the then frontier settlements of Pennsylvania, to a tract of excellent land lying on Marsh creek. At that place he cleared a large farm, and for seven or eight years enjoyed the fruits of his industry. Peace attended their labors; and they had nothing to alarm them, save the midnight howl of the prowling wolf, or the terrifying shriek of the ferocious panther, as they occasionally visited their improvements, to take a lamb or a calf to satisfy their hunger.

During this period my mother had two sons, between whose ages there was a difference of about three years: the oldest was named Matthew, and the other Robert.

Health presided on every countenance, and vigor and strength characterized every exertion. Our mansion was a little paradise. The morning of my childish, happy days, will ever stand fresh in my remembrance, notwithstanding the many severe trials through which I have passed, in arriving at my present situation, at so advanced an age. Even at this remote period, the recollection of my pleasant home at my father's, of my parents, of my brothers and sister, and of the manner in which I was deprived of them all at once, affects me so powerfully, that I am almost overwhelmed with grief, that is seemingly insupportable. Frequently I dream of those happy days: but, alas! they are gone: they have left me to be carried through a long life, dependent for the little pleasures of nearly seventy years, upon the tender mercies of the Indians! In the spring of 1752, and through the succeeding seasons, the stories of Indian barbarities inflicted upon the whites in those days, frequently excited in my parents the most serious alarm for our safety.

The next year the storm gathered faster; many murders were committed; and many captives were exposed to meet death in its most frightful form, by having their bodies stuck full of pine splinters, which were immediately set on fire, while their tormentors, exulting in their distress, would rejoice at their agony!

In 1754, an army for the protection of the settlers, and to drive back the French and Indians, was raised from the militia of the colonial governments, and placed (secondarily) under the command of Col. George Washington. In that army I had an uncle, whose name was John Jemison, who was killed at the battle at the Great Meadows, or Fort Necessity. His wife had died some time before this, and left a young child, which my mother nursed in the most tender manner, till its mother's sister took it away, a few months after my uncle's death. The

French and Indians, after the surrender of Fort Necessity by
Col. Washington, (which happened the same season, and
soon after his victory over them at that place,) grew more
and more terrible. The death of the whites, and plundering
and burning their property, was apparently their only object:
But as yet we had not heard the death-yell, nor seen the
smoke of a dwelling that had been lit by an Indian's hand.

The return of a new-year's day found us unmolested; and
though we knew that the enemy was at no great distance from
us, my father concluded that he would continue to occupy
his land another season; expecting (probably from the great
exertions which the government was then making) that as
soon as the troops could commence their operations in the
spring, the enemy would be conquered and compelled to
agree to a treaty of peace.

In the preceding autumn my father either moved to another part of his farm, or to another neighborhood, a short
distance from our former abode. I well recollect moving, and
that the barn that was on the place we moved to was built of
logs, though the house was a good one.

The winter of 1754–5 was as mild as a common fall season,
and the spring presented a pleasant seed time, and indicated
a plenteous harvest. My father, with the assistance of his
oldest sons, repaired his farm as usual, and was daily preparing the soil for the reception of the seed. His cattle and sheep
were numerous, and according to the best idea of wealth that
I can now form, he was wealthy.

But alas! how transitory are all human affairs! how fleeting
are riches! how brittle the invisible thread on which all earthly
comforts are suspended! Peace in a moment can take an
immeasurable flight; health can lose its rosy cheeks; and life
will vanish like a vapor at the appearance of the sun! In one
fatal day our prospects were all blasted; and death, by cruel
hands, inflicted upon almost the whole of the family.

On a pleasant day in the spring of 1755, when my father
was sowing flax-seed, and my brothers driving the teams, I
was sent to a neighbor's house, a distance of perhaps a mile,
to procure a horse and return with it the next morning. I went
as I was directed. I was out of the house in the beginning of
the evening, and saw a sheet wide spread approaching towards me, in which I was caught (as I have ever since be-

lieved) and deprived of my senses! The family soon found me on the ground, almost lifeless, (as they said,) took me in, and made use of every remedy in their power for my recovery, but without effect till day-break, when my senses returned, and I soon found myself in good health, so that I went home with the horse very early in the morning.

The appearance of that sheet, I have ever considered as a forerunner of the melancholy catastrophe that so soon afterwards happened to our family: and my being caught in it, I believe, was ominous of my preservation from death at the time we were captured.

Her Education.—Captivity.—Journey to Fort Pitt.—Mother's
Farewell Address.—Murder of her Family.—Preparation of
the Scalps.—Indian Precautions.—Arrival at Fort Pitt, &c.

MY education had received as much attention from my parents, as their situation in a new country would admit of. I had been at school some, where I learned to read in a book that was about half as large as a Bible; and in the Bible I had read a little. I had also learned the Catechism, which I used frequently to repent to my parents, and every night, before I went to bed, I was obliged to stand up before my mother and repeat some words that I suppose was a prayer.

My reading, Catechism and prayers, I have long since forgotten; though for a number of the first years that I lived with the Indians, I repeated the prayers as often as I had an opportunity. After the revolutionary war, I remembered the names of some of the letters when I saw them; but have never read a word since I was taken prisoner. It is but a few years since a Missionary kindly gave me a Bible, which I am very fond of hearing my neighbors read to me, and should be pleased to learn to read it myself; but my sight has been for a number of years, so dim that I have not been able to distinguish one letter from another.

As I before observed, I got home with the horse very early in the morning, where I found a man that lived in our neighborhood, and his sister-in-law who had three children, one son and two daughters. I soon learned that they had come

66

there to live a short time; but for what purpose I cannot say. The woman's husband, however, was at that time in Washington's army, fighting for his country; and as her brother-in-law had a house she had lived with him in his absence. Their names I have forgotten.

Immediately after I got home, the man took the horse to go to his house after a bag of grain, and took his gun in his hand for the purpose of killing game, if he should chance to see any.—Our family, as usual, was busily employed about their common business. Father was shaving an axe-helve at the side of the house; mother was making preparations for breakfast;—my two oldest brothers were at work near the barn; and the little ones, with myself, and the woman and her three children, were in the house.

Breakfast was not yet ready, when we were alarmed by the discharge of a number of guns, that seemed to be near. Mother and the women before mentioned, almost fainted at the report, and every one trembled with fear. On opening the door, the man and horse lay dead near the house, having just been shot by the Indians.

I was afterwards informed, that the Indians discovered him at his own house with his gun, and pursued him to father's, where they shot him as I have related. They first secured my father, and then rushed into the house, and without the least resistance made prisoners of my mother, Robert, Matthew, Betsey, the woman and her three children, and myself, and then commenced plundering.

My two brothers, Thomas and John, being at the barn, escaped and went to Virginia, where my grandfather Erwin then lived, as I was informed by a Mr. Fields, who was at my house about the close of the revolutionary war.

The party that took us consisted of six Indians and four Frenchmen, who immediately commenced plundering, as I just observed, and took what they considered most valuable, consisting principally of bread, meal and meat. Having taken as much provision as they could carry, they set out with their prisoners in great haste, for fear of detection, and soon entered the woods. On our march that day, an Indian went behind us with a whip, with which he frequently lashed the children to make them keep up. In this manner we travelled till dark without a mouthful of food or a drop of water; although we had not eaten since the night before. Whenever the little children cried for water, the Indians would make them drink urine or go thirsty. At night they encamped in the woods without fire and without shelter, where we were watched with the greatest vigilance. Extremely fatigued, and very hungry, we were compelled to lie upon the ground supperless and without a drop of water to satisfy the cravings of our appetites. As in the day time, so the little ones were made to drink urine in the night if they cried for water. Fatigue alone brought us a little sleep for the refreshment of our weary limbs; and at the dawn of day we were again started on our march in the same order that we had proceeded on the day before. About sunrise we were halted, and the Indians gave us a full breakfast of provision that they had brought from my father's house. Each of us being very hungry, partook of this bounty of the Indians, except father, who was so much overcome with his situation—so much exhausted by anxiety and grief, that silent despair seemed fastened upon his countenance, and he could not be prevailed upon to refresh his sinking nature by the use of a morsel of food. Our repast being finished, we again resumed our march, and before noon passed a small fort that I heard my father say was called Fort Canagojigge.

That was the only time that I heard him speak from the time we were taken till we were finally separated the following night.

Towards evening we arrived at the border of a dark and dismal swamp, which was covered with small hemlocks, or some other evergreen, and other bushes, into which we were conducted; and having gone a short distance we stopped to encamp for the night.

Here we had some bread and meat for supper: but the dreariness of our situation, together with the uncertainty under which we all labored, as to our future destiny, almost deprived us of the sense of hunger, and destroyed our relish for food.

Mother, from the time we were taken, had manifested a great degree of fortitude, and encouraged us to support our troubles without complaining; and by her conversation seemed to make the distance and time shorter, and the way more smooth. But father lost all his ambition in the beginning of our trouble, and continued apparently lost to every care—absorbed in melancholy. Here, as before, she insisted on the necessity of our eating; and we obeyed her, but it was done with heavy hearts.

As soon as I had finished my supper, an Indian took off my shoes and stockings and put a pair of moccasins on my feet, which my mother observed; and believing that they would spare my life, even if they should destroy the other captives, addressed me as near as I can remember in the following words:—

"My dear little Mary, I fear that the time has arrived when we must be parted forever. Your life, my child, I think will be spared; but we shall probably be tomahawked here in this lonesome place by the Indians. O! how can I part with you my darling? What will become of my sweet little Mary? Oh! how can I think of your being continued in captivity without a hope of your being rescued? O that death had snatched you from my embraces in your infancy; the pain of parting then would have been pleasing to what it now is; and I should have seen the end of your troubles!—Alas, my dear! my heart bleeds at the thoughts of what awaits you; but, if you leave us, remember my child your own name, and the name of your father and mother. Be careful and not forget your English tongue. If you shall have an opportunity to get away from the Indians, don't try to escape; for if you do they will find and destroy you. Don't forget, my little daughter, the prayers that I have learned you—say them often; be a good child, and God will bless you. May God bless you my child, and make you comfortable and happy."

During this time, the Indians stripped the shoes and stockings from the little boy that belonged to the woman who was taken with us, and put moccasins on his feet, as they had done before on mine. I was crying. An Indian took the little boy and myself by the hand, to lead us off from the company, when my mother exclaimed, "Don't cry Mary—don't cry my child. God will bless you! Farewell—farewell!"

The Indian led us some distance into the bushes, or woods, and there lay down with us to spend the night. The recollection of parting with my tender mother kept me awake, while the tears constantly flowed from my eyes. A number of times in the night the little boy begged of me earnestly to run away with him and get clear of the Indians; but remembering the advice I had so lately received, and knowing the dangers to which we should be exposed, in travelling without a path and without a guide, through a wilderness unknown to us, I told him that I would not go, and persuaded him to lie still till morning.

Early the next morning the Indians and Frenchmen that we had left the night before, came to us; but our friends were left behind. It is impossible for any one to form a correct idea of what my feelings were at the sight of those savages, whom I supposed had murdered my parents and brothers, sister, and friends, and left them in the swamp to be devoured by wild beasts! But what could I do? A poor little defenseless girl; without the power or means of escaping; without a home to go to, even if I could be liberated; without a knowledge of the direction or distance to my former place of residence; and without a living friend to whom to fly for protection, I felt a kind of horror, anxiety, and dread, that, to me, seemed insupportable. I durst not cry—I durst not complain; and to inquire of them the fate of my friends (even if I could have mustered resolution) was beyond my ability, as I could not speak their language, nor they understand mine. My only relief was in silent stifled sobs.

My suspicions as to the fate of my parents proved too true; for soon after I left them they were killed and scalped, together with Robert, Matthew, Betsey, and the woman and her two children, and mangled in the most shocking manner.

Having given the little boy and myself some bread and meat for breakfast, they led us on as fast as we could travel, and one of them went behind and with a long staff, picked up all the grass and weeds that we trailed down by going over them. By taking that precaution they avoided detection; for each weed was so nicely placed in its natural position that no one would have suspected that we had passed that way. It is the custom of Indians when scouting, or on private expeditions, to step carefully and where no impression of their feet can be left—shunning wet or muddy ground. They seldom take hold of a bush or limb, and never break one; and by observing those precautions and that of setting up the weeds and grass which they necessary lop, they completely elude the sagacity of their pursuers, and escape that punishment which they are conscious they merit from the hand of justice.

After a hard day's march we encamped in a thicket, where the Indians made a shelter of boughs, and then built a good fire to warm and dry our benumbed limbs and clothing; for it had rained some through the day. Here we were again fed as before. When the Indians had finished their supper they took from their baggage a number of scalps and went about preparing them for the market, or to keep without spoiling, by straining them over small hoops which they prepared for that purpose, and then drying and scraping them by the fire. Having put the scalps, yet wet and bloody, upon the hoops, and stretched them to their full extent, they held them to the fire till they were partly dried and then with their knives commenced scraping off the flesh; and in that way they continued to work, alternately drying and scraping them, till they were dry and clean. That being done they combed the hair in the neatest manner, and then painted it and the edges of the scalps yet on the hoops, red. Those scalps I knew at the time must have been taken from our family by the color of the hair. My mother's hair was red; and I could easily distinguish my father's and the children's from each other. That sight was most appalling; yet, I was obliged to endure it without complaining.

In the course of the night they made me to understand that they should not have killed the family if the whites had not pursued them.

Mr. Fields, whom I have before mentioned, informed me that at the time we were taken, he lived in the vicinity of my father; and that on hearing of our captivity, the whole neighborhood turned out in pursuit of the enemy, and to deliver us if possible: but that their efforts were unavailing. They however pursued us to the dark swamp, where they found my father, his family and companions, stripped and mangled in the most inhuman manner: That from thence the march of the cruel monsters could not be traced in any direction; and that they returned to their homes with the melancholy tidings of our misfortunes, supposing that we had all shared in the massacre.

The next morning we went on; the Indian going behind

us and setting up the weeds as on the day before. At night we encamped on the ground in the open air, without a shelter or fire.

In the morning we again set out early, and travelled as on the two former days, though the weather was extremely uncomfortable, from the continual falling of rain and snow.

At night the snow fell fast, and the Indians built a shelter of boughs, and a fire, when we rested tolerably dry through that and two succeeding nights.

When we stopped, and before the fire was kindled, I was so much fatigued from running, and so far benumbed by the wet and cold, that I expected that I must fail and die before I could get warm and comfortable. The fire, however, soon restored the circulation, and after I had taken my supper I felt so that I rested well through the night.

On account of the storm, we were two days at that place. On one of those days, a party consisting of six Indians who had been to the frontier settlements, came to where we were, and brought with them one prisoner, a young white man who was very tired and dejected. His name I have forgotten.

Misery certainly loves company. I was extremely glad to see him, though I knew from his appearance, that his situation was as deplorable as mine, and that he could afford me no kind of assistance. In the afternoon the Indians killed a deer, which they dressed, and then roasted it whole; which made them a full meal. We were each allowed a share of their venison, and some bread, so that we made a good meal also.

Having spent three nights and two days at that place, and the storm having ceased, early in the morning the whole company, consisting of twelve Indians, four Frenchmen, the young man, the little boy and myself, moved on at a moderate pace without an Indian behind us to deceive our pursuers.

In the afternoon we came in sight of Fort Pitt (as it is now called,) where we were halted while the Indians performed some customs upon their prisoners which they deemed necessary. That fort was then occupied by the French and Indians, and was called Fort Du Quesue. It stood at the junction of the Monongahela, which is said to signify, in some of the Indian languages, the Falling-in-Banks,* and the

* Navigator.

Alleghany* rivers, where the Ohio river begins to take its name. The word O-hi-o, signifies bloody.

At the place where we halted, the Indians combed the hair of the young man, the boy and myself, and then painted our faces and hair red, in the finest Indian style. We were then conducted into the fort, where we received a little bread, and were then shut up and left to tarry alone through the night.

* The word Alleghenny, was derived from an ancient race of Indians called "Tallegawe." The Delaware Indians, instead of saying "Alleghenny," say "Allegawe," or "Allegawenink." Western Tour—p. 465.

3

She is given to two Squaws.—Her Journey down the Ohio.—Passes a Shawanee town where white men had just been burnt.—Arrives at the Seneca town.—Her Reception.—She is adopted.—Ceremony of Adoption.—Indian Custom.—Address.—She receives a new name.—Her Employment.—Retains her own and learns the Seneca Language.—Situation of the Town, &c.—Indians go on a Hunting Tour to Sciota and take her with them.—Returns.—She is taken to Fort Pitt, and then hurried back by her Indian Sisters.—Her hopes of Liberty destroyed.—Second Tour to Sciota.—Returns to Wiishto, &c.—Arrival of Prisoners.—Priscilla Ramsay.—Her Chain.—Mary marries a Delaware.—Her Affection for him.—Birth and Death of her first Child.—Her Sickness and Recovery.—Birth of Thomas Jemison.

THE night was spent in gloomy forebodings. What the result of our captivity would be, it was out of our power to determine or even imagine.—At times we could almost realize the approach of our masters to butcher and scalp us;—again we could nearly see the pile of wood kindled on which we were to be roasted; and then we would imagine ourselves at liberty: alone and defenseless in the forest, surrounded by wild beasts that were ready to devour us. The anxiety of our minds drove sleep from our eyelids; and it was with a dreadful hope and painful impatience that we waited for the morning to determine our fate.

The morning at length arrived, and our masters came early and let us out of the house, and gave the young man

74

and boy to the French, who immediately took them away. Their fate I never learned; as I have not seen nor heard of them since.

I was now left alone in the fort, deprived of my former companions, and of every thing that was near or dear to me but life. But it was not long before I was in some measure relieved by the appearance of two pleasant looking squaws of the Seneca tribe, who came and examined me attentively for a short time, and then went out. After a few minutes absence they returned with my former masters, who gave me to them to dispose of as they pleased.

The Indians by whom I was taken were a party of Shawanees, if I remember right, that lived, when at home, a long distance down the Ohio.

My former Indian masters, and the two squaws, were soon ready to leave the fort, and accordingly embarked; the Indians in a large canoe, and the two squaws and myself in a small one, and went down the Ohio.

When we set off, an Indian in the forward canoe took the scalps of my former friends, strung them on a pole that he placed upon his shoulder, and in that manner carried them, standing in the stern of the canoe, directly before us as we sailed down the river, to the town where the two squaws resided.

On our way we passed a Shawanee town, where I saw a number of heads, arms, legs, and other fragments of the bodies of some white people who had just been burnt. The parts that remained were hanging on a pole which was supported at each end by a crotch stuck in the ground, and were roasted or burnt black as a coal. The fire was yet burning; and the whole appearances afforded a spectacle so shocking, that, even to this day, my blood almost curdles in my veins when I think of them!

At night we arrived at a small Seneca Indian town, at the mouth of a small river, that was called by the Indians, in the Seneca language, She-nan-jee,* where the two Squaws to

---

* That town, according to the geographical description given by Mrs. Jemison, must have stood at the mouth of Indian Cross creek, which is about 76 miles by water, below Pittsburgh; or at the mouth of Indian Short creek, 87 miles below Pittsburgh, where the town of Warren now stands: But at which of those places I am unable to determine.

whom I belonged resided. There we landed, and the Indians went on; which was the last I ever saw of them.

Having made fast to the shore, the Squaws left me in the canoe while they went to their wigwam or house in the town, and returned with a suit of Indian clothing, all new, and very clean and nice. My clothes, though whole and good when I was taken, were now torn in pieces, so that I was almost naked. They first undressed me and threw my rags into the river; then washed me clean and dressed me in the new suit they had just brought, in complete Indian style; and then led me home and seated me in the center of their wigwam.

I had been in that situation but a few minutes, before all the Squaws in the town came in to see me. I was soon surrounded by them, and they immediately set up a most dismal howling, crying bitterly, and wringing their hands in all the agonies of grief for a deceased relative.

Their tears flowed freely, and they exhibited all the signs of real mourning. At the commencement of this scene, one of their number began, in a voice somewhat between speaking and singing, to recite some words to the following purport, and continued the recitation till the ceremony was ended; the company at the same time varying the appearance of their countenances, gestures and tone of voice, so as to correspond with the sentiments expressed by their leader:

"Oh our brother! Alas! He is dead—he has gone; he will never return! Friendless he died on the field of the slain, where his bones are yet lying unburied! Oh, who will not mourn his sad fate? No tears dropped around him; oh, no! No tears of his sisters were there! He fell in his prime, when his arm was most needed to keep us from danger! Alas! he has gone! and left us in sorrow, his loss to bewail: Oh where is his spirit? His spirit went naked, and hungry it wanders, and thirsty and wounded it groans to return! Oh helpless and wretched, our brother has gone! No blanket nor food to nourish and warm him; nor candles to light him, nor weapons of war:—Oh, none of those comforts had he! But well we remember his deeds!—The deer he could take on the chase! The panther shrunk back at the sight of his strength! His enemies fell at his feet! He was brave and courageous in war! As the fawn he was harmless: his friendship was ardent: his temper was gentle: his pity was great! Oh! our friend, our companion is dead! Our brother, our brother, alas! he is gone! But why do we grieve for his loss? In the strength of a warrior, undaunted he left us, to fight by the side of the Chiefs! His war-whoop was shrill! His rifle well aimed laid his enemies low: his tomahawk drank of their blood: and his knife flayed their scalps while yet covered with gore! And why do we mourn? Though he fell on the field of the slain, with glory he fell, and his spirit went up to the land of his fathers in war! Then why do we mourn? With transports of joy they received him, and fed him, and clothed him, and welcomed him there! Oh friends, he is happy; then dry up your tears! His spirit has seen our distress, and sent us a helper whom with pleasure we greet. Dickewamis has come: then let us receive her with joy! She is handsome and pleasant! Oh! she is our sister, and gladly we welcome her here. In the place of our brother she stands in our tribe. With care we will guard her from trouble; and may she be happy till her spirit shall leave us."

In the course of that ceremony, from mourning they became serene—joy sparkled in their countenances, and they seemed to rejoice over me as over a long lost child. I was made welcome amongst them as a sister to the two Squaws before mentioned, and was called Dickewamis; which being interpreted, signifies a pretty girl, a handsome girl, or a pleasant, good thing. That is the name by which I have ever since been called by the Indians.

I afterwards learned that the ceremony I at that time passed through, was that of adoption. The two squaws had lost a brother in Washington's war, sometime in the year before, and in consequence of his death went up to Fort Pitt, on the day on which I arrived there, in order to receive a prisoner or an enemy scalp, to supply their loss.

It is a custom of the Indians, when one of their number is slain or taken prisoner in battle, to give to the nearest relative to the dead or absent, a prisoner, if they have chanced to take one, and if not, to give him the scalp of an enemy. On the return of the Indians from conquest, which is always announced by peculiar shoutings, demonstrations of joy, and the exhibition of some trophy of victory, the mourners come forward and make their claims. If they receive a prisoner, it is at their option either to satiate their vengeance by taking his life in the most cruel manner they can conceive of; or, to receive and adopt him into the family, in the place of him whom they have lost. All the prisoners that are taken in battle and carried to the encampment or town by the Indians, are given to the bereaved families, till their number is made good. And unless the mourners have but just received the news of their bereavement, and are under the operation of paroxysm of grief, anger and revenge; or, unless the prisoner is very old, sickly, or homely, they generally save him, and treat him kindly. But if their mental wound is fresh, their loss so great that they deem it irreparable, or if their prisoner or prisoners do not meet their approbation, no torture, let it be ever so cruel, seems sufficient to make them satisfaction. It is family, and not national, sacrifices amongst the Indians, that has given them an indelible stamp as barbarians, and identified their character with the idea which is generally formed of unfeeling ferocity, and the most abandoned cruelty.

It was my happy lot to be accepted for adoption; and at the time of the ceremony I was received by the two squaws, to supply the place of their brother in the family; and I was ever considered and treated by them as a real sister, the same as though I had been born of their mother.

During my adoption, I sat motionless, nearly terrified to death at the appearance and actions of the company, expecting every moment to feel their vengeance, and suffer death on the spot. I was, however, happily disappointed, when at the close of the ceremony the company retired, and my sisters went about employing every means for my consolation and comfort.

Being now settled and provided with a home, I was employed in nursing the children, and doing light work about the house. Occasionally I was sent out with the Indian hunters, when they went but a short distance, to help them carry their game. My situation was easy; I had no particular hardships to endure. But still, the recollection of my parents, my brothers and sisters, my home, and my own captivity, destroyed my happiness, and made me constantly solitary, lonesome and gloomy.

My sisters would not allow me to speak English in their hearing; but remembering the charge that my dear mother gave me at the time I left her, whenever I chanced to be alone I made a business of repeating my prayer, catechism, or something I had learned in order that I might not forget my own language. By practicing in that way I retained it till I came to Genesee flats, where I soon became acquainted with English people with whom I have been almost daily in the habit of conversing.

My sisters were diligent in teaching me their language; and to their great satisfaction I soon learned so that I could understand it readily, and speak it fluently. I was very fortunate in falling into their hands; for they were kind good natured women; peaceable and mild in their dispositions; temperate and decent in their habits, and very tender and gentle towards me. I have great reason to respect them, though they have been dead a great number of years.

The town where they lived was pleasantly situated on the Ohio, at the mouth of the Shenanjee; the land produced good corn; the woods furnished a plenty of game, and the waters abounded with fish. Another river emptied itself into the Ohio, directly opposite the mouth of the Shenanjee. We spent the summer at that place, where we planted, hoed, and harvested a large crop of corn, of an excellent quality.

About the time of corn harvest, Fort Pitt was taken from the French by the English.*

The corn being harvested, the Indians took it on horses and in canoes, and proceeded down the Ohio, occasionally stopping to hunt a few days, till we arrived at the mouth of Sciota river; where they established their winter quarters, and continued hunting till the ensuing spring, in the adjacent wilderness. While at that place I went with the other children to assist the hunters to bring in their game. The forests on the Sciota were well stocked with elk, deer, and other large animals; and the marshes contained large numbers of beaver, muskrat, &c. which made excellent hunting for the Indians;

---

* The above statement is apparently an error; and is to be attributed solely to the treachery of the old lady's memory; though she is confident that that event took place at the time above mentioned. It is certain that Fort Pitt was not evacuated by the French and given up to the English, till sometime in November 1758. It is possible, however, that an armistice was agreed upon, and that for a time, between the spring of 1755 and 1758, both nations visited that post without fear of molestation. As the succeeding part of the narrative corresponds with the true historical chain of events, the public will overlook this circumstance, which appears unsupported by history.

who depended, for their meat, upon their success in taking elk and deer; and for ammunition and clothing, upon the beaver, muskrat, and other furs that they could take in addition to their peltry.

The season for hunting being passed, we all returned in the spring to the mouth of the river Shenanjee, to the houses and fields we had left in the fall before. There we again planted our corn, squashes, and beans, on the fields that we occupied the preceding summer.

About planting time, our Indians all went up to Fort Pitt, to make peace with the British, and took me with them.* We landed on the opposite side of the river from the fort, and encamped for the night. Early the next morning the Indians took me over to the fort to see the white people that were there. It was then that my heart bounded to be liberated from the Indians and to be restored to my friends and my country. The white people were surprised to see me with the Indians, enduring the hardships of a savage life, at so early an age, and with so delicate a constitution as I appeared to possess. They asked me my name; where and when I was taken—and appeared very much interested on my behalf. They were continuing their inquiries, when my sisters became alarmed, believing that I should be taken from them, hurried me into their canoe and recrossed the river—took their bread out of the fire and fled with me, without stopping, till they arrived at the river Shenanjee. So great was their fear of losing me, or of my being given up in the treaty, that they never once stopped rowing till they got home.

Shortly after we left the shore opposite the fort, as I was informed by one of my Indian brothers, the white people came over to take me back; but after considerable inquiry, and having made diligent search to find where I was hid, they returned with heavy hearts. Although I had then been with the Indians something over a year, and had become considerably habituated to their mode of living, and attached to my sisters, the sight of white people who could speak English inspired me with an unspeakable anxiety to go home with

*History is silent as to any treaty having been made between the English, and French and Indians, at that time; though it is possible that a truce was agreed upon, and that the parties met for the purpose of concluding a treaty of peace.

them, and share in the blessings of civilization. My sudden departure and escape from them, seemed like a second captivity, and for a long time I brooded the thoughts of my miserable situation with almost as much sorrow and dejection as I had done those of my first sufferings. Time, the destroyer of every affection, wore away my unpleasant feelings, and I became as contented as before.

We tended our cornfields through the summer; and after we had harvested the crop, we again went down the river to the hunting ground on the Sciota, where we spent the winter, as we had done the winter before.

Early in the spring we sailed up the Ohio river, to a place that the Indians called Wiishto,* where one river emptied into the Ohio on one side, and another on the other. At that place the Indians built a town, and we planted corn.

We lived three summers at Wiishto, and spent each winter on the Sciota.

The first summer of our living at Wiishto, a party of Delaware Indians came up the river, took up their residence, and lived in common with us. They brought five white prisoners with them, who by their conversation, made my situation much more agreeable, as they could all speak English. I have forgotten the names of all of them except one, which was Priscilla Ramsay. She was a very handsome, good natured girl, and was married soon after she came to Wiishto to Capt. Little Billy's uncle, who went with her on a visit to her friends in the states. Having tarried with them as long as she wished to, she returned with her husband to Can-a-ah-tua, where he died. She, after his death, married a white man by the name of Nettles, and now lives with him (if she is living) on Grand River, Upper Canada.

Not long after the Delawares came to live with us, at Wiishto, my sisters told me that I must go and live with one of them, whose name was She-nin-jee. Not daring to cross them, or disobey their commands, with a great degree of reluctance I went; and Sheninjee and I were married according to Indian custom.

---

*Wiishto I suppose was situated near the mouth of Indian Guyundat, 327 miles below Pittsburgh, and 73 above Big Sciota; or at the mouth of Swan creek, 307 miles below Pittsburgh.

Sheninjee was a noble man; large in stature; elegant in his appearance; generous in his conduct; courageous in war; a friend to peace, and a great lover of justice. He supported a degree of dignity far above his rank, and merited and received the confidence and friendship of all the tribes with whom he was acquainted. Yet, Sheninjee was an Indian. The idea of spending my days with him, at first seemed perfectly irreconcilable to my feelings: but his good nature, generosity, tenderness, and friendship towards me, soon gained my affection; and, strange as it may seem, I loved him!—To me he was ever kind in sickness, and always treated me with gentleness; in fact, he was an agreeable husband, and a comfortable companion. We lived happily together till the time of our final separation, which happened two or three years after our marriage, as I shall presently relate.

In the second summer of my living at Wiishto, I had a child at the time that the kernels of corn first appeared on the cob. When I was taken sick, Sheninjee was absent, and I was sent to a small shed, on the bank of the river, which was made of boughs, where I was obliged to stay till my husband returned. My two sisters, who were my only companions, attended me, and on the second day of my confinement my child was born; but it lived only two days. It was a girl: and notwithstanding the shortness of the time that I possessed it, it was a great grief to me to lose it.

After the birth of my child, I was very sick, but was not allowed to go into the house for two weeks; when, to my great joy, Sheninjee returned, and I was taken in and as comfortably provided for as our situation would admit of. My disease continued to increase for a number of days; and I became so far reduced that my recovery was despaired of by my friends, and I concluded that my troubles would soon be finished. At length, however, my complaint took a favorable turn, and by the time that the corn was ripe I was able to get about. I continued to gain my health, and in the fall was able to go to our winter quarters, on the Sciota, with the Indians.

From that time, nothing remarkable occurred to me till the fourth winter of my captivity, when I had a son born, while I was at Sciota: I had a quick recovery, and my child was healthy. To commemorate the name of my much lamented father, I called my son Thomas Jemison.

4

She leaves Wiishto for Fort Pitt, in company with her Husband.—
Her feelings on setting out.—Contrast between the labor of the
white and Indian Women.—Deficiency of Arts amongst the
Indians.—Their former Happiness.—Baneful effects of Civilization, and the introduction of ardent Spirits amongst them.
&c.—Journey up the River.—Murder of three Traders by the
Shawnees.—Her Husband stops at a Trading House.—Wantonness of the Shawnees.—Moves up the Sandusky.— Meets
her Brother from Ge-nish-a-u.—Her Husband goes to Wiishto,
and she sets out for Genishau in company with her Brothers.—
They arrive at Sandusky.—Occurrences at that place.—Her
Journey to Genishau, and Reception by Her Mother and
Friends.

IN the spring, when Thomas was three or four moons
[months] old, we returned from Sciota to Wiishto, and soon
after set out to go to Fort Pitt, to dispose of our fur and skins,
that we had taken in the winter, and procure some necessary
articles for the use of our family.

I had then been with the Indians four summers and four
winters, and had become so far accustomed to their mode of
living, habits and dispositions, that my anxiety to get away,
to be set at liberty, and leave them, had almost subsided.
With them was my home; my family was there, and there I
had many friends to whom I was warmly attached in consideration of the favors, affection and friendship with which they
had uniformly treated me, from the time of my adoption. Our
labor was not severe; and that of one year was exactly similar,

in almost every respect, to that of the others, without that endless variety that is to be observed in the common labor of the white people. Notwithstanding the Indian women have all the fuel and bread to procure, and the cooking to perform, their task is probably not harder than that of white women, who have those articles provided for them; and their cares certainly are not half as numerous, nor as great. In the summer season, we planted, tended and harvested our corn, and generally had all our children with us; but had no master to oversee or drive us, so that we could work as leisurely as we pleased. We had no ploughs on the Ohio; but performed the whole process of planting and hoeing with a small tool that resembled, in some respects, a hoe with a very short handle.

Our cooking consisted in pounding our corn into samp or hommany, boiling the hommany, making now and then a cake and baking it in the ashes, and in boiling or roasting our venison. As our cooking and eating utensils consisted of a hommany block and pestle, a small kettle, a knife or two, and a few vessels of bark or wood, it required but little time to keep them in order for use.

Spinning, weaving, sewing, stocking knitting, and the like, are arts which have never been practiced in the Indian tribes generally. After the revolutionary war, I learned to sew, so that I could make my own clothing after a poor fashion; but the other domestic arts I have been wholly ignorant of the application of, since my captivity. In the season of hunting, it was our business, in addition to our cooking, to bring home the game that was taken by the Indians, dress it, and carefully preserve the eatable meat, and prepare or dress the skins. Our clothing was fastened together with strings of deer skin, and tied on with the same.

In that manner we lived, without any of those jealousies, quarrels, and revengeful battles between families and individuals, which have been common in the Indian tribes since the introduction of ardent spirits amongst them.

The use of ardent spirits amongst the Indians and the attempts which have been made to civilize and christianize them by the white people, has constantly made them worse and worse; increased their vices, and robbed them of many of their virtues; and will ultimately produce their extermination. I have seen, in a number of instances, the effects of education upon some of our Indians, who were taken when young, from their families, and placed at school before they had had an opportunity to contract many Indian habits, and there kept till they arrived to manhood, but I have never seen one of those but what was an Indian in every respect after he returned. Indians must and will be Indians, in spite of all the means that can be used for their cultivation in the sciences and arts.

One thing only marred my happiness, while I lived with them on the Ohio; and that was the recollection that I had once had tender parents and a home that I loved. Aside from that consideration, or, if I had been taken in infancy, I should have been contented in my situation. Notwithstanding all that has been said against the Indians, in consequence of their cruelties to their enemies—cruelties that I have witnessed, and had abundant proof of—it is a fact that they are naturally kind, tender and peaceable towards their friends, and strictly honest; and that those cruelties have been practised, only upon their enemies, according to their idea of justice.

At the time we left Wiishto, it was impossible for me to suppress a sigh of regret on parting with those who had truly been my friends—with those whom I had every reason to respect. On account of a part of our family living at Genishau, we thought it doubtful whether we should return directly from Pittsburgh, or go from thence on a visit to see them.

Our company consisted of my husband, my two Indian brothers, my little son and myself. We embarked in a canoe that was large enough to contain ourselves and our effects, and proceeded on our voyage up the river.

Nothing remarkable occurred to us on our way, till we arrived at the mouth of a creek which Sheninjee and my brothers said was the outlet of Sandusky lake; where, as they said, two or three English traders in fur and skins had kept a trading house but a short time before, though they were then absent. We had passed the trading house but a short distance, when we met three white men floating down the river, with the appearance of having been recently murdered by the Indians. We supposed them to be the bodies of the traders, whose store we had passed the same day. Sheninjee being alarmed for fear of being apprehended as one of the murderers, if he should go on, resolved to put about immedi-

ately, and we accordingly returned to where the traders had
lived, and there landed.

At the trading house we found a party of Shawnee Indians,
who had taken a young white man prisoner, and had just
begun to torture him for the sole purpose of gratifying their
curiosity in exulting at his distress. They at first made him
stand up, while they slowly pared his ears and split them into
strings; they then made a number of slight incisions in his
face; and then bound him upon the ground, rolled him in the
dirt, and rubbed it in his wounds: some of them at the same
time whipping him with small rods! The poor fellow cried for
mercy and yelled most piteously.

The sight of his distress seemed too much for me to endure: I begged of them to desist—I entreated them with tears
to release him. At length they attended to my intercessions,
and set him at liberty. He was shockingly disfigured, bled
profusely, and appeared to be in great pain; but as soon as
he was liberated he made off in haste, which was the last I
saw of him.

We soon learned that the same party of Shawnees had,
but a few hours before, massacred the three white traders
whom we saw in the river, and had plundered their store.
We, however, were not molested by them, and after a short
stay at that place, moved up the creek about forty miles to a
Shawnee town, which the Indians called Gaw-gush-shaw-ga,
(which being interpreted signifies a mask or a false face.) The
creek that we went up was called Candusky.

It was now summer; and having tarried a few days at
Gawgushshawga, we moved on up the creek to a place that
was called Yis-kah-wa-na, (meaning in English open mouth.)

As I have before observed, the family to which I belonged
was part of a tribe of Seneca Indians, who lived, at that time,
at a place called Genishau, from the name of the tribe, that
was situated on a river of the same name which is now called
Genesee. The word Genishaw signifies a shining, clear or
open place. Those of us who lived on the Ohio, had frequently
received invitations from those at Genishau, by one of my
brothers, who usually went and returned every season, to
come and live with them, and my two sisters had been gone
almost two years.

While we were at Yiskahwana, my brother arrived there

from Genishau, and insisted so strenuously upon our going home (as he called it) with him, that my two brothers concluded to go, and to take me with them.

By this time the summer was gone, and the time for harvesting corn had arrived. My brothers, for fear of the rainy season setting in early, thought it best to set out immediately that we might have good travelling. Sheninjee consented to have me go with my brothers; but concluded to go down the river himself with some fur and skins which he had on hand, spend the winter in hunting with his friends, and come to me in the spring following.

That was accordingly agreed upon, and he set out for Wiishto; and my three brothers and myself, with my little son on my back, at the same time set out for Genishau. We came on to Upper Sandusky, to an Indian town that we found deserted by its inhabitants, in consequence of their having recently murdered some English traders, who resided amongst them. That town was owned and had been occupied by Delaware Indians, who, when they left it, buried their provision in the earth, in order to preserve it from their enemies, or to have a supply for themselves if they should chance to return. My brothers understood the customs of the Indians when they were obliged to fly from their enemies; and suspecting that their corn at least must have been hid, made diligent search, and at length found a large quantity of it, together with beans, sugar and honey, so carefully buried that it was completely dry and as good as when they left it. As our stock of provision was scanty, we considered ourselves extremely fortunate in finding so seasonable a supply, with so little trouble. Having caught two or three horses, that we found there, and furnished ourselves with a good store of food, we travelled on till we came to the mouth of French Creek, where we hunted two days, and from thence came on to Conowongo Creek, where we were obliged to stay seven or ten days, in consequence of our horses having left us and straying into the woods. The horses, however, were found, and we again prepared to resume our journey. During our stay at that place the rain fell fast, and had raised the creek to such a height that it was seemingly impossible for us to cross it. A number of times we ventured in, but were compelled to return, barely escaping with our lives. At length we succeeded in swimming our horses and reached the opposite shore; though I but just escaped with my little boy from being drowned. From Sandusky the path that we travelled was crooked and obscure; but was tolerably well understood by my oldest brother, who had travelled it a number of times, when going to and returning from the Cherokee wars. The fall by this time was considerably advanced, and the rains, attended with cold winds, continued daily to increase the difficulties of travelling. From Conowongo we came to a place, called by the Indians Che-ua-shung-gau-tau, and from that to U-na-waum-gwa, (which means an eddy, not strong), where the early frosts had destroyed the corn so that the Indians were in danger of starving for the want of bread. Having rested ourselves two days at that place, we came on to Caneadea and stayed one day, and then continued our march till we arrived at Genishau. Genishau at that time was a large Seneca town, thickly inhabited, lying on Genesee river, opposite what is now called the Free Ferry, adjoining Fall-Brook, and about south west of the present village of Geneseo, the county seat for the county of Livingston, in the state of New-York.

Those only who have travelled on foot the distance of five or six hundred miles, through an almost pathless wilderness, can form an idea of the fatigue and sufferings that I endured on that journey. My clothing was thin and illy calculated to defend me from the continually drenching rains with which I was daily completely wet, and at night with nothing but my wet blanket to cover me, I had to sleep on the naked ground, and generally without a shelter, save such as nature had provided. In addition to all that, I had to carry my child, then about nine months old, every step of the journey on my back, or in my arms, and provide for his comfort and prevent his suffering, as far as my poverty of means would admit. Such was the fatigue that I sometimes felt, that I thought it impossible for me to go through, and I would almost abandon the idea of even trying to proceed. My brothers were attentive, and at length, as I have stated, we reached our place of destination, in good health, and without having experienced a day's sickness from the time we left Yiskahwana.

We were kindly received by my Indian mother and the other members of the family, who appeared to make me welcome; and my two sisters, whom I had not seen in two years, received me with every expression of love and friendship, and that they really felt what they expressed, I have never had the least reason to doubt. The warmth of their feelings, the kind reception which I met with, and the continued favors that I received at their hands, rivitted my affection for them so strongly that I am constrained to believe that I loved them as I should have loved my own sister had she lived, and I had been brought up with her.

5

Indians march to Niagara to fight the British.—Return with two
Prisoners, &c.—Sacrifice them at Fall-Brook.—Her Indian
Mother's Address to her Daughter.—Death of her Husband.—
Bounty offered for the Prisoners taken in the last war.—John
Van Sice attempts to take her to procure her Ransom.—Her
Escape.—Edict of the Chiefs.—Old King of the tribe deter-
mines to have her given up.—Her brother threatens her Life.—
Her narrow Escape—The old King goes off.—Her brother is
informed of the place of her concealment, and conducts her
home.—Marriage to her second Husband.—Names of her
Children.

WHEN we arrived at Genishau, the Indians of that tribe
were making active preparations for joining the French, in
order to assist them in retaking Fort Ne-a-gaw (as Fort Niagara was called in the Seneca language) from the British, who
had taken it from the French in the month preceding. They
marched off the next day after our arrival, painted and accou-
tred in all the habiliments of Indian warfare, determined on
death or victory; and joined the army in season to assist in
accomplishing a plan that had been previously concerted for
the destruction of a part of the British army. The British
feeling themselves secure in the possession of Fort Neagaw,
and unwilling that their enemies should occupy any of the
military posts in that quarter, determined to take Fort Schlos-
ser, lying a few miles up the river from Neagaw, which
they expected to effect with but little loss. Accordingly a
detachment of soldiers, sufficiently numerous, as was sup-

90

posed, was sent out to take it, leaving a strong garrison in the fort, and marched off, well prepared to effect their object. But on their way they were surrounded by the French and Indians, who lay in ambush to receive them, and were driven off the bank of the river into a place called the "Devil's Hole," together with their horses, carriages, artillery, and every thing pertaining to the army. Not a single man escaped being driven off, and of the whole number one only was fortunate enough to escape with his life. Our Indians were absent but a few days, and returned in triumph, bringing with them two white prisoners, and a number of oxen. Those were the first neat cattle that were ever brought to the Genesee flats.

The next day after their return to Genishau, was set apart as a day of feasting and frolicing, at the expence of the lives of their two unfortunate prisoners, on whom they purposed to glut their revenge, and satisfy their love for retaliation upon their enemies. My sister was anxious to attend the execution, and to take me with her, to witness the customs of the warriors, as it was one of the highest kind of frolics ever celebrated in their tribe, and one that was not often attended with so much pomp and parade as it was expected that would be. I felt a kind of anxiety to witness the scene, having never attended an execution, and yet I felt a kind of horrid dread that made my heart revolt, and inclined me to step back rather than support the idea of advancing. On the morning of the execution she made her intention of going to the frolic, and taking me with her, known to our mother, who in the most feeling terms remonstrated against a step at once so rash and unbecoming the true dignity of our sex:

"How, my daughter, (said she, addressing my sister,) how can you even think of attending the feast and seeing the unspeakable torments that those poor unfortunate prisoners must inevitably suffer from the hands of our warriors? How can you stand and see them writhing in the warriors' fire, in all the agonies of a slow, a lingering death? How can you think of enduring the sound of their groanings and prayers to the Great Spirit for sudden deliverance from their enemies, or from life? And how can you think of conducting to that melancholy spot your poor sister Dickewamis, (meaning myself,) who has so lately been a prisoner, who has lost her parents and brothers by the hands of the bloody warriors, and who has felt all the horrors of the loss of her freedom, in lonesome captivity? Oh! how can you think of making her bleed at the wounds which are now but partially healed? The recollection of her former troubles would deprive us of Dickewamis, and she would depart to the fields of the blessed, where fighting has ceased, and the corn needs no tending— where hunting is easy, the forests delightful, the summers are pleasant, and the winters are mild!—O! think once, my daughter, how soon you may have a brave brother made prisoner in battle, and sacrificed to feast the ambition of the enemies of his kindred, and leave us to mourn for the loss of a friend, a son and a brother, whose bow brought us venison, and supplied us with blankets!—Our task is quite easy at home, and our business needs our attention. With war we have nothing to do: our husbands and brothers are proud to defend us, and their hearts beat with ardor to meet our proud foes. Oh! stay then, my daughter; let our warriors alone perform on their victims their customs of war!"

This speech of our mother had the desired effect; we stayed at home and attended to our domestic concerns. The prisoners, however, were executed by having their heads taken off, their bodies cut in pieces and shockingly mangled, and then burnt to ashes!—They were burnt on the north side of Fall-brook, directly opposite the town which was on the south side, some time in the month of November, 1759.

I spent the winter comfortably, and as agreeably as I could have expected to, in the absence of my kind husband. Spring at length appeared, but Sheninjee was yet away; summer came on, but my husband had not found me. Fearful forebodings haunted my imagination; yet I felt confident that his affection for me was so great that if he was alive he would follow me and I should again see him. In the course of the summer, however, I received intelligence that soon after he left me at Yiskahwana he was taken sick and died at Wiishto. This was a heavy and an unexpected blow. I was now in my youthful days left a widow, with one son, and entirely dependent on myself for his and my support. My mother and her family gave me all the consolation in their power, and in a few months my grief wore off and I became contented.

In a year or two after this, according to my best recollection of the time, the King of England offered a bounty to those who would bring in the prisoners that had been taken in the war, to some military post where they might be redeemed and set at liberty.

John Van Sice, a Dutchman, who had frequently been at our place, and was well acquainted with every prisoner at Genishau, resolved to take me to Niagara, that I might there receive my liberty and he the offered bounty. I was notified of his intention; but as I was fully determined not to be redeemed at that time, especially with his assistance, I carefully watched his movements in order to avoid falling into his hands. It so happened, however, that he saw me alone at work in a corn-field, and thinking probably that he could secure me easily, ran towards me in great haste. I espied him at some distance, and well knowing the amount of his errand, ran from him with all the speed I was mistress of, and never once stopped till I reached Gardow.* He gave up the chase, and returned: but I, fearing that he might be lying in wait for me, stayed three days and three nights in an old cabin at Gardow, and then went back trembling at every step for fear of being apprehended. I got home without difficulty; and soon after, the chiefs in council having learned the cause of my elopement, gave orders that I should not be taken to any military post without my consent; and that as it was my choice to stay, I should live amongst them quietly and undisturbed. But, notwithstanding the will of the chiefs, it was but a few days before the old king of our tribe told one of my Indian brothers that I should be redeemed, and he would take me to Niagara himself. In reply to the old king, my brother said that I should not be given up; but that, as it was my wish, I should stay with the tribe as long as I was pleased to. Upon this a serious quarrel ensued between them, in which my brother frankly told him that sooner than I should be taken by force, he would kill me with his own hands!—Highly enraged at the old king, my brother came to my sister's house, where I resided, and informed her of all that had passed respecting me; and that, if the old king should attempt to take me, as he firmly believed he would, he would immediately take my life, and hazard the consequences. He returned to

---

* I have given this orthography, because it corresponds with the popular pronunciation.

the old king. As soon as I came in, my sister told me what she had just heard, and what she expected without doubt would befal me. Full of pity, and anxious for my preservation, she then directed me to take my child and go into some high weeds at no great distance from the house, and there hide myself and lay still till all was silent in the house, for my brother, she said, would return at evening and let her know the final conclusion of the matter, of which she promised to inform me in the following manner: If I was to be killed, she said she would bake a small cake and lay it at the door, on the outside, in a place that she then pointed out to me. When all was silent in the house, I was to creep softly to the door, and if the cake could not be found in the place specified, I was to go in: but if the cake was there, I was to take my child and go as fast as I possibly could to a large spring on the south side of Samp's Creek, (a place that I had often seen,) and there wait till I should by some means hear from her.

Alarmed for my own safety, I instantly followed her advice, and went into the weeds, where I lay in a state of the greatest anxiety, till all was silent in the house, when I crept to the door, and there found, to my great distress, the little cake! I knew my fate was fixed, unless I could keep secreted till the storm was over; and accordingly crept back to the weeds, where my little Thomas lay, took him on my back, and laid my course for the spring as fast as my legs would carry me. Thomas was nearly three years old, and very large and heavy. I got to the spring early in the morning, almost overcome with fatigue, and at the same time fearing that I might be pursued and taken, I felt my life an almost insupportable burden. I sat down with my child at the spring, and he and I made a breakfast of the little cake, and water of the spring, which I dipped and supped with the only implement which I possessed, my hand.

In the morning after I fled, as was expected, the old King came to our house in search of me, and to take me off; but, as I was not to be found, he gave me up, and went to Niagara with the prisoners he had already got into his possession.

As soon as the old King was fairly out of the way, my sister told my brother where he could find me. He immediately set out for the spring, and found me about noon. The first sight of him made me tremble with the fear of death; but when he came near, so that I could discover his countenance, tears of joy flowed down my cheeks, and I felt such a kind of instant relief as no one can possibly experience, unless when under the absolute sentence of death he receives an unlimited pardon. We were both rejoiced at the event of the old King's project; and after staying at the spring through the night, set out together for home early in the morning. When we got to a cornfield near the town, my brother secreted me till he could go and ascertain how my case stood; and finding that the old King was absent, and that all was peaceable, he returned to me, and I went home joyfully.

Not long after this, my mother went to Johnstown, on the Mohawk river, with five prisoners, who were redeemed by Sir William Johnson, and set at liberty.

When my son Thomas was three or four years old, I was married to an Indian, whose name was Hiokatoo, commonly called Gardow, by whom I had four daughters and two sons. I named my children, principally, after my relatives, from whom I was parted, by calling my girls Jane, Nancy, Betsey and Polly, and the boys John and Jesse. Jane died about twenty-nine years ago, in the month of August, a little before the great Council at Big-Tree, aged about fifteen years. My other daughters are yet living, and have families.

6

Peace amongst the Indians.—Celebrations.—Worship. Exercises.—Business of the Tribes.—Former Happiness of the Indians in time of peace extolled.—Their Morals; Fidelity; Honesty; Chastity; Temperance. Indians called to German Flats.—Treaty with Americans.—They are sent for by the British Commissioners, and go to Oswego.—Promises made by those Commissioners.—Greatness of the King of England. Reward that was paid them for joining the British. They make a Treaty.—Bounty offered for Scalps. Return richly dressed and equipped.—In 1776 they kill a man at Cautega to provoke the Americans. Prisoners taken at Cherry Valley, brought to Beard's Town; redeemed, &c.—Battle at Fort Stanwix.—Indians suffer a great loss.—Mourning at Beard's Town.—Mrs. Jemison's care of and services rendered to Butler and Brandt.

AFTER the conclusion of the French war, our tribe had nothing to trouble it till the commencement of the Revolution. For twelve or fifteen years the use of the implements of war was not known, nor the war-whoop heard, save on days of festivity, when the achievements of former times were commemorated in a kind of mimic warfare, in which the chiefs and warriors displayed their prowess, and illustrated their former adroitness, by laying the ambuscade, surprizing their enemies, and performing many accurate manoeuvres with the tomahawk and scalping knife; thereby preserving and handing to their children, the theory of Indian warfare. During that period they also pertinaciously observed the religious rites of their progenitors, by attending with the most scrupulous exactness and a great degree of enthusiasm to the sacrifices, at particular times, to appease the anger of the evil deity, or to excite the commisseration and friendship of the Great Good Spirit, whom they adored with reverence, as the author, governor, supporter and disposer of every good thing of which they participated.

They also practised in various athletic games, such as running, wrestling, leaping, and playing ball, with a view that their bodies might be more supple, or rather that they might not become enervated, and that they might be enabled to make a proper selection of Chiefs for the councils of the nation and leaders for war.

While the Indians were thus engaged in their round of traditionary performances, with the addition of hunting, their women attended to agriculture, their families, and a few domestic concerns of small consequence, and attended with but little labor.

No people can live more happy than the Indians did in times of peace, before the introduction of spirituous liquors amongst them. Their lives were a continual round of pleasures. Their wants were few, and easily satisfied; and their cares were only for to-day; the bounds of their calculations for future comfort not extending to the incalculable uncertainties of to-morrow. If peace ever dwelt with men, it was in former times, in the recesses from war, amongst what are now termed barbarians. The moral character of the Indians was (if I may be allowed the expression) uncontaminated. Their fidelity was perfect, and became proverbial; they were strictly honest; they despised deception and falsehood; and chastity was held in high veneration, and a violation of it was considered sacrilege. They were temperate in their desires, moderate in their passions, and candid and honorable in the expression of their sentiments on every subject of importance.

Thus, at peace amongst themselves, and with the neighboring whites, though there were none at that time very near, our Indians lived quietly and peaceably at home, till a little before the breaking out of the revolutionary war, when they were sent for, together with the Chiefs and members of the Six Nations generally, by the people of the States, to go to the German Flats, and there hold a general council, in order that the people of the states might ascertain, in good season, who they should esteem and treat as enemies, and who as friends, in the great war which was upon the point of breaking out between them and the King of England.

Our Indians obeyed the call, and the council was holden, at which the pipe of peace was smoked, and a treaty made, in which the Six Nations solemnly agreed that if a war should eventually break out, they would not take up arms on either side; but that they would observe a strict neutrality. With that the people of the states were satisfied, as they had not asked their assistance, nor did not wish it. The Indians returned to their homes well pleased that they could live on neutral ground, surrounded by the din of war, without being engaged in it.

About a year passed off, and we, as usual, were enjoying ourselves in the employments of peaceable times, when a messenger arrived from the British Commissioners, requesting all the Indians of our tribe to attend a general council which was soon to be held at Oswego. The council convened, and being opened, the British Commissioners informed the Chiefs that the object of calling a council of the Six Nations, was, to engage their assistance in subduing the rebels, the people of the states, who had risen up against the good King, their master, and were about to rob him of a great part of his possessions and wealth, and added that they would amply reward them for all their services.

The Chiefs then arose, and informed the Commissioners of the nature and extent of the treaty which they had entered into with the people of the states, the year before, and that they should not violate it by taking up the hatchet against them.

The Commissioners continued their entreaties without success, till they addressed their avarice, by telling our people that the people of the states were few in number, and easily subdued; and that on the account of their disobedience to the King, they justly merited all the punishment that it was possible for white men and Indians to inflict upon them; and added, that the King was rich and powerful, both in money and subjects: That his rum was as plenty as the water in lake Ontario: that his men were as numerous as the sands upon the lake shore:—and that the Indians, if they would assist in the war, and persevere in their friendship to the King, till it was closed, should never want for money or goods. Upon this the Chiefs concluded a treaty with the British Commissioners, in which they agreed to take up arms against the rebels, and continue in the service of his Majesty till they were subdued, in consideration of certain conditions which were stipulated in the treaty to be performed by the British government and its agents.

As soon as the treaty was finished, the Commissioners made a present to each Indian of a suit of clothes, a brass kettle, a gun and tomahawk, a scalping knife, a quantity of powder and lead, a piece of gold, and promised a bounty on every scalp that should be brought in. Thus richly clad and equipped, they returned home, after an absence of about two weeks, full of the fire of war, and anxious to encounter their enemies. Many of the kettles which the Indians received at that time are now in use on the Genesee Flats.

Hired to commit depredations upon the whites, who had given them no offence, they waited impatiently to commence their labor, till sometime in the spring of 1776, when a convenient opportunity offered for them to make an attack. At that time, a party of our Indians were at Cau-te-ga, who shot a man that was looking after his horse, for the sole purpose, as I was informed by my Indian brother, who was present, of commencing hostilities.

In May following, our Indians were in their first battle with the Americans; but at what place I am unable to determine. While they were absent at that time, my daughter Nancy was born.

The same year, at Cherry Valley, our Indians took a woman and her three daughters prisoners, and brought them on, leaving one at Canandaigua, one at Honeoy, one at Cattaraugus, and one (the woman) at Little Beard's Town, where I resided. The woman told me that she and her daughters might have escaped, but that they expected the British army only, and therefore made no effort. Her husband and sons got away. Sometime having elapsed, they were redeemed at Fort Niagara by Col. Butler, who clothed them well and sent them home.

In the same expedition, Joseph Smith was taken prisoner at or near Cherry Valley, brought to Genesee, and detained till after the revolutionary war. He was then liberated, and the Indians made him a present, in company with Horatio Jones, of 6000 acres of land lying in the present town of Leicester, in the county of Livingston.

One of the girls just mentioned, was married to a British officer at Fort Niagara, by the name of Johnson, who at the time she was taken, took a gold ring from her finger, without any compliments or ceremonies. When he saw her at Niagara he recognized her features, restored the ring that he had so impolitely borrowed, and courted and married her.

Previous to the battles at Fort Stanwix, the British sent for the Indians to come and see them whip the rebels; and, at the same time stated that they did not wish to have them fight, but wanted to have them just sit down, smoke their pipes, and look on. Our Indians went, to a man; but contrary to their expectation, instead of smoking and looking on, they were obliged to fight for their lives, and in the end of the battle were completely beaten, with a great loss in killed and wounded. Our Indians alone had thirty-six killed, and a great number wounded. Our town exhibited a scene of real sorrow and distress, when our warriors returned and recounted their misfortunes, and stated the real loss they had sustained in the engagement. The mourning was excessive, and was expressed by the most doleful yells, shrieks, and howlings, and by inimitable gesticulations.

During the revolution, my house was the home of Col's Butler and Brandt, whenever they chanced to come into our neighborhood as they passed to and from Fort Niagara, which was the seat of their military operations. Many and many a night I have pounded samp for them from sun-set till sunrise, and furnished them with necessary provision and clean clothing for their journey.

7

Gen. Sullivan with a large army arrives at Canandaigua.—Indians'
troubles.—Determine to stop their march.—Skirmish at Connessius Lake.—Circumstances attending the Execution of an
Oneida warrior. Escape of an Indian Prisoner.—Lieut. Boyd
and another man taken Prisoners.—Cruelty of Boyd's Execution.—Indians retreat to the woods.—Sullivan comes on to
Genesee Flats and destroys the property of the Indians.—
Returns.—Indians return.—Mrs. Jemison goes to Gardow.—
Her Employment there.—Attention of an old Negro to her
safety, &c.—Severe Winter.—Sufferings of the Indians.—Destruction of Game.—Indians' Expedition to the Mohawk.—
Capture old John O'Bail, &c.—Other Prisoners taken, &c.

FOR four or five years we sustained no loss in the war, except
in the few who had been killed in distant battles; and our
tribe, because of the remoteness of its situation from the
enemy, felt secure from an attack. At length, in the fall of
1779, intelligence was received that a large and powerful
army of the rebels, under the command of General Sullivan,
was making rapid progress towards our settlement, burning
and destroying the huts and corn-fields; killing the cattle,
hogs and horses, and cutting down the fruit trees belonging
to the Indians throughout the country.

Our Indians immediately became alarmed, and suffered
every thing but death from fear that they should be taken by
surprize, and totally destroyed at a single blow. But in order
to prevent so great a catastrophe, they sent out a few spies
who were to keep themselves at a short distance in front of

the invading army, in order to watch its operations, and give information of its advances and success.

Sullivan arrived at Canandaigua Lake, and had finished his work of destruction there, and it was ascertained that he was about to march to our flats when our Indians resolved to give him battle on the way, and prevent, if possible, the distresses to which they knew we should be subjected, if he should succeed in reaching our town. Accordingly they sent all their women and children into the woods a little west of Little Beard's Town, in order that we might make a good retreat if it should be necessary, and then, well armed, set out to face the conquering enemy. The place which they fixed upon for their battle ground lay between Honeoy Creek and the head of Connessius Lake.

At length a scouting party from Sullivan's army arrived at the spot selected, when the Indians arose from their ambush with all the fierceness and terror that it was possible for them to exercise, and directly put the party upon a retreat. Two Oneida Indians were all the prisoners that were taken in that skirmish. One of them was a pilot of Gen. Sullivan, and had been very active in the war, rendering to the people of the states essential services. At the commencement of the revolution he had a brother older than himself, who resolved to join the British service, and endeavored by all the art that he was capable of using to persuade his brother to accompany him; but his arguments proved abortive. This went to the British, and that joined the American army. At this critical juncture they met, one in the capacity of a conqueror, the other in that of a prisoner; and as an Indian seldom forgets a countenance that he has seen, they recognized each other at sight. Envy and revenge glared in the features of the conquering savage, as he advanced to his brother (the prisoner) in all the haughtiness of Indian pride, heightened by a sense of power, and addressed him in the following manner:

"Brother, you have merited death! The hatchet or the war-club shall finish your career!—When I begged of you to follow me in the fortunes of war, you was deaf to my cries— you spurned my entreaties!

"Brother! you have merited death and shall have your deserts! When the rebels raised their hatchets to fight their good master, you sharpened your knife, you brightened your rifle and led on our foes to the fields of our fathers!— You have merited death and shall die by our hands! When those rebels had drove us from the fields of our fathers to seek out new homes, it was you who could dare to step forth as their pilot, and conduct them even to the doors of our wigwams, to butcher our children and put us to death! No crime can be greater!—But though you have merited death and shall die on this spot, my hands shall not be stained in the blood of a brother! *Who will strike?"*

Little Beard, who was standing by, as soon as the speech was ended, struck the prisoner on the head with his toma-hawk, and despatched him at once!

Little Beard then informed the other Indian prisoner that as they were at war with the whites only, and not with the Indians, they would spare his life, and after a while give him his liberty in an honorable manner. The Oneida warrior, however, was jealous of Little Beard's fidelity; and suspecting that he should soon fall by his hands, watched for a favorable opportunity to make his escape; which he soon effected. Two Indians were leading him, one on each side, when he made a violent effort, threw them upon the ground, and ran for his life towards where the main body of the American army was encamped. The Indians pursued him without success; but in their absence they fell in with a small detachment of Sullivan's men, with whom they had a short but severe skirmish, in which they killed a number of the enemy, took Capt. or Lieut. William Boyd and one private, prisoners, and brought them to Little Beard's Town, where they were soon after put to death in the most shocking and cruel manner. Little Beard, in this, as in all other scenes of cruelty that happened at his town, was master of ceremonies, and principal actor. Poor Boyd was stripped of his clothing, and then tied to a sapling, where the Indians menaced his life by throwing their toma-hawks at the tree, directly over his head, brandishing their scalping knives around him in the most frightful manner, and accompanying their ceremonies with terrific shouts of joy. Having punished him sufficiently in this way, they made a small opening in his abdomen, took out an intestine, which they tied to the sapling, and then unbound him from the tree, and drove him around it till he had drawn out the whole of his intestines. He was then beheaded, his head was stuck upon a pole, and his body left on the ground unburied. Thus ended the life of poor William Boyd, who, it was said, had every appearance of being an active and enterprizing officer, of the first talents. The other prisoner was (if I remember distinctly) only beheaded and left near Boyd.

This tragedy being finished, our Indians again held a short council on the expediency of giving Sullivan battle, if he should continue to advance, and finally came to the conclusion that they were not strong enough to drive him, nor to prevent his taking possession of their fields: but that if it was possible they would escape with their own lives, preserve their families, and leave their possessions to be overrun by the invading army.

The women and children were then sent on still further towards Buffalo, to a large creek that was called by the Indians Catawba, accompanied by a part of the Indians, while the remainder secreted themselves in the woods back of Beard's Town, to watch the movements of the army.

At that time I had three children who went with me on foot, one who rode on horse back, and one whom I carried on my back.

Our corn was good that year; a part of which we had gathered and secured for winter.

In one or two days after the skirmish at Connissius lake, Sullivan and his army arrived at Genesee river, where they destroyed every article of the food kind that they could lay their hands on. A part of our corn they burnt, and threw the remainder into the river. They burnt our houses, killed what few cattle and horses they could find, destroyed our fruit trees, and left nothing but the bare soil and timber. But the Indians had eloped and were not to be found.

Having crossed and recrossed the river, and finished the work of destruction, the army marched off to the east. Our Indians saw them move off, but suspecting that it was Sullivan's intention to watch our return, and then to take us by surprise, resolved that the main body of our tribe should hunt where we then were, till Sullivan had gone so far that there would be no danger of his returning to molest us.

This being agreed to, we hunted continually till the Indians concluded that there could be no risk in our once more taking possession of our lands. Accordingly we all returned;

but what were our feelings when we found that there was not a mouthful of any kind of sustenance left, not even enough to keep a child one day from perishing with hunger.

The weather by this time had become cold and stormy; and as we were destitute of houses and food too, I immediately resolved to take my children and look out for myself, without delay. With this intention I took two of my little ones on my back, bade the other three follow, and the same night arrived on the Gardow flats, where I have ever since resided.

At that time, two negroes, who had run away from their masters sometime before, were the only inhabitants of those flats. They lived in a small cabin and had planted and raised a large field of corn, which they had not yet harvested. As they were in want of help to secure their crop, I hired to them to husk corn till the whole was harvested.

I have laughed a thousand times to myself when I have thought of the good old negro, who hired me, who fearing that I should get taken or injured by the Indians, stood by me constantly when I was husking, with a loaded gun in his hand, in order to keep off the enemy, and thereby lost as much labor of his own as he received from me, by paying good wages. I, however, was not displeased with his attention; for I knew that I should need all the corn that I could earn, even if I should husk the whole. I husked enough for them, to gain for myself, at every tenth string, one hundred strings of ears, which were equal to twenty-five bushels of shelled corn. This seasonable supply made my family comfortable for samp and cakes through the succeeding winter, which was the most severe that I have witnessed since my remembrance. The snow fell about five feet deep, and remained so for a long time, and the weather was extremely cold; so much so indeed, that almost all the game upon which the Indians depended for subsistence, perished, and reduced them almost to a state of starvation through that and three or four succeeding years. When the snow melted in the spring, deer were found dead upon the ground in vast numbers; and other animals, of every description, perished from the cold also, and were found dead, in multitudes. Many of our people barely escaped with their lives, and some actually died of hunger and freezing.

But to return from this digression: Having been completely routed at Little Beard's Town, deprived of a house, and without the means of building one in season, after I had finished my husking, and having found from the short acquaintance which I had had with the negroes, that they were kind and friendly, I concluded, at their request, to take up my residence with them for a while in their cabin, till I should be able to provide a hut for myself. I lived more comfortably than I expected to through the winter, and the next season made a shelter for myself.

The negroes continued on my flats two or three years after this, and then left them for a place that they expected would suit them much better. But as that land became my own in a few years, by virtue of a deed from the Chiefs of the Six Nations, I have lived there from that to the present time.

My flats were cleared before I saw them; and it was the opinion of the oldest Indians that were at Genishau, at the time that I first went there, that all the flats on the Genesee river were improved before any of the Indian tribes ever saw them. I well remember that soon after I went to Little Beard's Town, the banks of Fall-Brook were washed off, which left a large number of human bones uncovered. The Indians then said that those were not the bones of Indians, because they had never heard of any of their dead being buried there; but that they were the bones of a race of men who a great many moons before, cleared that land and lived on the flats.

The next summer after Sullivan's campaign, our Indians, highly incensed at the whites for the treatment they had received, and the sufferings which they had consequently endured, determined to obtain some redress by destroying their frontier settlements. Corn Planter, otherwise called John O'Bail, led the Indians, and an officer by the name of Johnston commanded the British in the expedition. The force was large, and so strongly bent upon revenge and vengeance, that seemingly nothing could avert its march, nor prevent its depredations. After leaving Genesee they marched directly to some of the head waters of the Susquehannah river, and Schoharie Creek, went down that creek to the Mohawk river, thence up that river to Fort Stanwix, and from thence came home. In their route they burnt a number of places; destroyed all the cattle and other property that fell in their way; killed a number of white people, and brought home a few prisoners.

In that expedition, when they came to Fort Plain, on the Mohawk river, Corn Planter and a party of his Indians took old John O'Bail, a white man, and made him a prisoner. Old John O'Bail, in his younger days had frequently passed through the Indian settlements that lay between the Hudson and Fort Niagara, and in some of his excursions had become enamored with a squaw, by whom he had a son that was called Corn Planter.

Corn Planter, was a chief of considerable eminence; and having been informed of his parentage and of the place of his father's residence, took the old man at this time, in order that he might make an introduction leisurely, and become acquainted with a man to whom, though a stranger, he was satisfied that he owed his existence.

After he had taken the old man, his father, he led him as a prisoner ten or twelve miles up the river, and then stepped before him, faced about, and addressed him in the following terms:—

"My name is John O'Bail, commonly called Corn Planter. I am your son! you are my father! You are now my prisoner, and subject to the customs of Indian warfare: but you shall not be harmed; you need not fear. I am a warrior! Many are the scalps which I have taken! Many prisoners I have tortured to death! I am your son! I am a warrior! I was anxious to see you, and to greet you in friendship. I went to your cabin and took you by force! But your life shall be spared. Indians love their friends and their kindred, and treat them with kindness. If now you choose to follow the fortune of your yellow son, and to live with our people, I will cherish your old age with plenty of venison, and you shall live easy: But if it is your choice to return to your fields and live with your white children, I will send a party of my trusty young men to conduct you back in safety. I respect you, my father; you have been friendly to Indians, and they are your friends."

Old John chose to return. Corn Planter, as good as his word, ordered an escort to attend him home, which they did with the greatest of care.

Amongst the prisoners that were brought to Genesee, was William Newkirk, a man by the name of Price, and two negroes.

Price lived a while with Little Beard, and afterwards with

Jack Berry, an Indian. When he left Jack Berry he went to Niagara, where he now resides.

Newkirk was brought to Beard's Town, and lived with Little Beard and at Fort Niagara about one year, and then enlisted under Butler, and went with him on an expedition to the Monongahela.

8

Life of Ebenezer Allen, a Tory.—He comes to Gardow.—His inti-
macy with a Nanticoke Squaw.—She gives him a Cap.—Her
Husband's jealousy.—Cruelty to his Wife.—Hiokatoo's Man-
date.—Allen supports her.—Her Husband is received into favor.—Allen labors.—Purchases Goods.—Stops the Indian
War.—His troubles with the Indians.—Marries a Squaw.—Is
taken and carried to Quebec.—Acquitted.—Goes to Philadelphia.—Returns to Genesee with a Store of Goods, &c.—Goes
to Farming.—Moves to Allen's Creek.—Builds Mills at Rochester.—Drowns a Dutchman.—Marries a white Wife.—Kills
an old Man.—Gets a Concubine.—Moves to Mt. Morris.—
Marries a third Wife and gets another Concubine.—Receives
a tract of Land.—Sends his Children to other States, &c.—
Disposes of his Land.—Moves to Grand River, where he
dies.—His Cruelties.

SOMETIME near the close of the revolutionary war, a white
man by the name of Ebenezer Allen, left his people in the
state of Pennsylvania on the account of some disaffection
towards his countrymen, and came to the Genesee river, to
reside with the Indians. He tarried at Genishau a few days,
and came up to Gardow, where I then resided.—He was,
apparently, without any business that would support him; but
he soon became acquainted with my son Thomas, with whom
he hunted for a long time, and made his home with him at
my house; winter came on, and he continued his stay.

When Allen came to my house, I had a white man living
on my land, who had a Nanticoke squaw for his wife, with

109

whom he had lived very peaceably; for he was a moderate man commonly, and she was a kind, gentle, cunning creature. It so happened that he had no hay for his cattle; so that in the winter he was obliged to drive them every day, perhaps a half mile from his house, to let them feed on rushes, which in those days were so numerous as to nearly cover the ground.

Allen having frequently seen the squaw in the fall, took the opportunity when her husband was absent with his cows, daily to make her a visit; and in return for his kindnesses she made and gave him a red cap finished and decorated in the highest Indian style.

The husband had for some considerable length of time felt a degree of jealousy that Allen was trespassing upon him with the consent of his squaw; but when he saw Allen dressed in so fine an Indian cap, and found that his dear Nanticoke had presented it to him, his doubts all left him, and he became so violently enraged that he caught her by the hair of her head, dragged her on the ground to my house, a distance of forty rods, and threw her in at the door. Hiokatoo, my husband, exasperated at the sight of so much inhumanity, hastily took down his old tomahawk, which for awhile had lain idle, shook it over the cuckold's head, and bade him jogo (i.e. go off.) The enraged husband, well knowing that he should feel a blow if he waited to hear the order repeated, instantly retreated, and went down the river to his cattle. We protected the poor Nanticoke woman, and gave her victuals; and Allen sympathized with her in her misfortunes till spring, when her husband came to her, acknowledged his former errors, and that he had abused her without a cause, promised a reformation, and she received him with every mark of a renewal of her affection. They went home lovingly, and soon after removed to Niagara.

The same spring, Allen commenced working my flats, and continued to labor there till after the peace in 1783. He then went to Philadelphia on some business that detained him but a few days, and returned with a horse and some dry goods, which he carried to a place that is now called Mount Morris, where he built or bought a small house.

The British and Indians on the Niagara frontier, dissatisfied with the treaty of peace, were determined, at all hazards, to continue their depredations upon the white settlements which lay between them and Albany. They actually made ready, and were about setting out on an expedition to that effect, when Allen (who by this time understood their customs of war) took a belt of wampum, which he had fraudulently procured, and carried it as a token of peace from the Indians to the commander of the nearest American military post.

The Indians were soon answered by the American officer that the wampum was cordially accepted; and, that a continuance of peace was ardently wished for. The Indians, at this, were chagrined and disappointed beyond measure; but as they held the wampum to be a sacred thing, they dared not to go against the import of its meaning, and immediately buried the hatchet as it respected the people of the United States; and smoked the pipe of peace. They, however, resolved to punish Allen for his officiousness in meddling with their national affairs, by presenting the sacred wampum without their knowledge, and went about devising means for his detection. A party was accordingly despatched from Fort Niagara to apprehend him; with orders to conduct him to that post for trial, or for safe keeping, till such time as his fate should be determined upon in a legal manner.

The party came on; but before it arrived at Gardow, Allen got news of its approach, and fled for safety, leaving the horse and goods that he had brought from Philadelphia, an easy prey to his enemies. He had not been long absent when they arrived at Gardow, where they made diligent search for him till they were satisfied that they could not find him, and then seized the effects which he had left, and returned to Niagara. My son Thomas, went with them, with Allen's horse, and carried the goods.

Allen, on finding that his enemies had gone, came back to my house, where he lived as before; but of his return they were soon notified at Niagara, and Nettles (who married Priscilla Ramsay) with a small party of Indians came on to take him. He, however, by some means found that they were near, and gave me his box of money and trinkets to keep safely, till he called for it, and again took to the woods.

Nettles came on determined at all events to take him before he went back; and, in order to accomplish his design, he, with his Indians, hunted in the day time and lay by at night at my house, and in that way they practised for a number of days. Allen watched the motion of his pursuers, and every night after they had gone to rest, came home and got some food, and then returned to his retreat. It was in the fall, and the weather was cold and rainy, so that he suffered extremely. Some nights he sat in my chamber till nearly day-break, while his enemies were below, and when the time arrived I assisted him to escape unnoticed.

Nettles at length abandoned the chase—went home, and Allen, all in tatters, came in. By running in the woods his clothing had become torn into rags, so that he was in a suffer-ing condition, almost naked. Hiokatoo gave him a blanket, and a piece of broadcloth for a pair of trowsers. Allen made his trowsers himself, and then built a raft, on which he went down the river to his own place at Mount Morris.

About that time he married a squaw, whose name was Sally.

The Niagara people finding that he was at his own house, came and took him by surprize when he least expected them, and carried him to Niagara. Fortunately for him, it so hap-pened that just as they arrived at the fort, a house took fire and his keepers all left him to save the building, if possible. Allen had supposed his doom to be nearly sealed; but finding himself at liberty he took to his heels, left his escort to put out the fire, and ran to Tonnawanta. There an Indian gave him some refreshment, and a good gun, with which he has-tened on to Little Beard's Town, where he found his squaw. Not daring to risk himself at that place for fear of being given up, he made her but a short visit, and came immediately to Gardow.

Just as he got to the top of the hill above the Gardow flats, he discovered a party of British soldiers and Indians in pursuit of him; and in fact they were so near that he was satisfied that they saw him, and concluded that it would be impossible for him to escape. The love of liberty, however, added to his natural swiftness, gave him sufficient strength to make his escape to his former castle of safety. His pursuers came imme-diately to my house, where they expected to have found him secreted, and under my protection. They told me where they had seen him but a few moments before, and that they were confident that it was within my power to put him into their hands. As I was perfectly clear of having had any hand in his escape, I told them plainly that I had not seen him since he was taken to Niagara, and that I could give them no information at all respecting him. Still unsatisfied, and doubting my veracity, they advised my Indian brother to use his influence to draw from me the secret of his concealment, which they had an idea that I considered of great importance, not only to him but to myself. I persisted in my ignorance of his situation, and finally they left me.

Although I had not seen Allen, I knew his place of security, and was well aware that if I told them the place where he had formerly hid himself, they would have no difficulty in making him a prisoner.

He came to my house in the night, and awoke me with the greatest caution, fearing that some of his enemies might be watching to take him at a time when, and in a place where it would be impossible for him to make his escape. I got up and assured him that he was then safe; but that his enemies would return early in the morning and search him out if it should be possible. Having given him some victuals, which he received thankfully, I told him to go, but to return the next night to a certain corner of the fence near my house where he would find a quantity of meal that I would have well prepared and deposited there for his use.

Early the next morning, Nettles and his company came in while I was pounding the meal for Allen, and insisted upon my giving him up. I again told them that I did not know where he was, and that I could not, neither would I, tell them any thing about him. I well knew that Allen considered his life in my hands; and although it was my intention not to lie, I was fully determined to keep his situation a profound secret. They continued their labor and examined (as they supposed) every crevice, gully, tree and hollow log in the neighboring woods, and at last concluded that he had left the country, and gave him up for lost, and went home.

At that time Allen lay in a secret place in the gulph a short distance above my flats, in a hole that he accidentally found in the rock near the river. At night he came and got the meal at the corner of the fence as I had directed him, and afterwards lived in the gulph two weeks. Each night he came to the pasture and milked one of my cows, without any other vessel in which to receive the milk than his hat, out of which

he drank it. I supplied him with meal, but fearing to build a
fire he was obliged to eat it raw and wash it down with
the milk. Nettles having left our neighborhood, and Allen
considering himself safe, left his little cave and came home.
I gave him his box of money and trinkets, and he went to his
own house at Mount Morris. It was generally considered by
the Indians of our tribe, that Allen was an innocent man, and
that the Niagara people were persecuting him without a just
cause. Little Beard, then about to go to the eastward on public
business, charged his Indians not to meddle with Allen, but
to let him live amongst them peaceably, and enjoy himself
with his family and property if he could. Having the protection of the chief, he felt himself safe, and let his situation be
known to the whites from whom he suspected no harm. They,
however, were more inimical than our Indians and were
easily bribed by Nettles to assist in bringing him to justice.
Nettles came on, and the whites, as they had agreed, gave
poor Allen up to him. He was bound and carried to Niagara,
where he was confined in prison through the winter. In the
spring he was taken to Montreal or Quebec for trial, and was
honorably acquitted. The crime for which he was tried was,
for his having carried the wampum to the Americans, and
thereby putting too sudden a stop to their war.

From the place of his trial he went directly to Philadelphia, and purchased on credit, a boat load of goods which he
brought by water to Conhocton, where he left them and came
to Mount Morris for assistance to get them brought on. The
Indians readily went with horses and brought them to his
house, where he disposed of his dry goods; but not daring to
let the Indians begin to drink strong liquor, for fear of the
quarrels which would naturally follow, he sent his spirits to
my place and we sold them. For his goods he received ginseng
roots, principally, and a few skins. Ginseng at that time was
plenty, and commanded a high price. We prepared the whole
that he received for the market, expecting that he would
carry them to Philadelphia. In that I was disappointed; for
when he had disposed of, and got pay for all his goods, he
took the ginseng and skins to Niagara, and there sold them
and came home.

Tired of dealing in goods, he planted a large field of
corn on or near his own land, attended to it faithfully, and

succeeded in raising a large crop, which he harvested, loaded into canoes and carried down the river to the mouth of Allen's Creek, then called by the Indians Gin-is-a-ga, where he unloaded it, built him a house, and lived with his family.

The next season he planted corn at that place and built a grist and saw mill on Genesee Falls, now called Rochester.

At the time Allen built the mills, he had an old German living with him by the name of Andrews, whom he sent in a canoe down the river with his mill irons. Allen went down at the same time; but before they got to the mills Allen threw the old man overboard and drowned him, as it was then generally believed, for he was never seen or heard of afterwards.

In the course of the season in which Allen built his mills, he became acquainted with the daughter of a white man, who was moving to Niagara. She was handsome, and Allen soon got into her good graces, so that he married and took her home, to be a joint partner with Sally, the squaw, whom she had never heard of till she got home and found her in full possession; but it was too late for her to retrace the hasty steps she had taken, for her father had left her in the care of a tender husband and gone on. She, however, found that she enjoyed at least an equal half of her husband's affections, and made herself contented. Her father's name I have forgotten, but her's was Lucy.

Allen was not contented with two wives, for in a short time after he had married Lucy he came up to my house, where he found a young woman who had an old husband with her. They had been on a long journey, and called at my place to recruit and rest themselves. She filled Allen's eye, and he accordingly fixed upon a plan to get her into his possession. He praised his situation, enumerated his advantages, and finally persuaded them to go home and tarry with him a few days at least, and partake of a part of his comforts. They accepted his generous invitation and went home with him. But they had been there but two or three days when Allen took the old gentleman out to view his flats; and as they were deliberately walking on the bank of the river, pushed him into the water. The old man, almost strangled, succeeded in getting out; but his fall and exertions had so powerful an effect upon his system that he died in two or three days, and left his young widow to the protection of his murderer. She lived with him about one year in a state of concubinage and then left him.

How long Allen lived at Allen's Creek I am unable to state; but soon after the young widow left him, he removed to his old place at Mount Morris, and built a house, where he made Sally, his squaw, by whom he had two daughters, a slave to Lucy, by whom he had had one son; still, however, he considered Sally to be his wife.

After Allen came to Mt. Morris at that time, he married a girl by the name of Morilla Gregory, whose father at the time lived on Genesee Flats. The ceremony being over, he took her home to live in common with his other wives; but his house was too small for his family; for Sally and Lucy, conceiving that their lawful privileges would be abridged if they received a partner, united their strength and whipped poor Morilla so cruelly that he was obliged to keep her in a small Indian house a short distance from his own, or lose her entirely. Morilla, before she left Mt. Morris, had four children.

One of Morilla's sisters lived with Allen about a year after Morilla was married, and then quit him.

A short time after they all got to living at Mt. Morris, Allen prevailed upon the Chiefs to give to his Indian children, a tract of land four miles square, where he then resided. The Chiefs gave them the land, but he so artfully contrived the conveyance, that he could apply it to his own use, and by alienating his right, destroy the claim of his children.

Having secured the land, in that way, to himself, he sent his two Indian girls to Trenton, (N.J.) and his white son to Philadelphia, for the purpose of giving each of them a respectable English education.

While his children were at school, he went to Philadelphia, and sold his right to the land which he had begged of the Indians for his children to Robert Morris. After that, he sent for his daughters to come home, which they did.

Having disposed of the whole of his property on the Genesee river, he took his two white wives and their children, together with his effects, and removed to a Delaware town on the river De Trench, in Upper Canada. When he left Mt. Morris, Sally, his squaw, insisted upon going with him, and actually followed him, crying bitterly, and praying for his protection some two or three miles, till he absolutely bade her leave him, or he would punish her with severity.

At length, finding her case hopeless, she returned to the Indians.

At the great treaty at Big Tree, one of Allen's daughters claimed the land which he had sold to Morris. The claim was examined and decided against her in favor of Ogden, Trumbull, Rogers and others, who were the creditors of Robert Morris. Allen yet believed that his daughter had an indisputable right to the land in question, and got me to go with mother Farly, a half Indian woman, to assist him by interceding with Morris for it, and to urge the propriety of her claim. We went to Thomas Morris, and having stated to him our business, he told us plainly that he had no land to give away, and that as the title was good, he never would allow Allen, nor his heirs, one foot, or words to that effect. We returned to Allen the answer we had received, and he, conceiving all further attempts to be useless, went home.

He died at the Delaware town, on the river De Trench, in the year 1814 or 15, and left two white widows and one squaw, with a number of children, to lament his loss.

By his last will he gave all his property to his last wife, (Morilla,) and her children, without providing in the least for the support of Lucy, or any of the other members of his family. Lucy, soon after his death, went with her children down the Ohio river, to receive assistance from her friends.

In the revolutionary war, Allen was a tory, and by that means became acquainted with our Indians, when they were in the neighborhood of his native place, desolating the settlements on the Susquehannah. In those predatory battles, he joined them, and (as I have often heard the Indians say,) for cruelty was not exceeded by any of his Indian comrades!

At one time, when he was scouting with the Indians in the Susquehannah country, he entered a house very early in the morning, where he found a man, his wife, and one child, in bed. The man, as he entered the door, instantly sprang on the floor, for the purpose of defending himself and little family; but Allen dispatched him at one blow. He then cut off his head and threw it bleeding into the bed with the terrified woman; took the little infant from its mother's breast, and holding it by its legs, dashed its head against the jamb, and left the unhappy widow and mother to mourn alone over her murdered family. It has been said by some, that after he had killed the child, he opened the fire and buried it under the coals and embers: But of that I am not certain. I have often heard him speak of that transaction with a great degree of sorrow, and as the foulest crime he had ever committed—one for which I have no doubt he repented.

9

Mrs. Jemison has liberty to go to her Friends.—Chooses to stay.—
Her Reasons, &c.—Her Indian Brother makes provision for
her Settlement.—He goes to Grand River and dies.—Her love
for him, &c.—She is presented with the Gardow Reservation.—
Is troubled by Speculators.—Description of the Soil, &c. of
her Flats.—Indian notions of the ancient Inhabitants of this
Country.

SOON after the close of the revolutionary war, my Indian
brother, Kau-jises-tau-ge-au (which being interpreted signifies Black Coals), offered me my liberty, and told me that if
it was my choice I might go to my friends.

My son, Thomas, was anxious that I should go; and offered to go with me and assist me on the journey, by taking
care of the younger children, and providing food as we travelled through the wilderness. But the Chiefs of our tribe,
suspecting from his appearance, actions, and a few warlike
exploits, that Thomas would be a great warrior, or a good
counsellor, refused to let him leave them on any account
whatever.

To go myself, and leave him, was more than I felt able to
do; for he had been kind to me, and was one on whom I
placed great dependence. The Chiefs refusing to let him go,
was one reason for my resolving to stay; but another, more
powerful, if possible, was, that I had got a large family of
Indian children, that I must take with me; and that if I should
be so fortunate as to find my relatives, they would despise

119

them, if not myself; and treat us as enemies; or, at least with a degree of cold indifference, which I thought I could not endure.

Accordingly, after I had duly considered the matter, I told my brother that it was my choice to stay and spend the remainder of my days with my Indian friends, and live with my family as I had heretofore done. He appeared well pleased with my resolution, and informed me, that as that was my choice, I should have a piece of land that I could call my own, where I could live unmolested, and have something at my decease to leave for the benefit of my children.

In a short time he made himself ready to go to Upper Canada; but before he left us, he told me that he would speak to some of the Chiefs at Buffalo, to attend the great Council, which he expected would convene in a few years at farthest, and convey to me such a tract of land as I should select. My brother left us, as he had proposed, and soon after died at Grand River.

Kaujisestaugeau, was an excellent man, and ever treated me with kindness. Perhaps no one of his tribe at any time exceeded him in natural mildness of temper, and warmth and tenderness of affection. If he had taken my life at the time when the avarice of the old King inclined him to procure my emancipation, it would have been done with a pure heart and from good motives. He loved his friends; and was generally beloved. During the time that I lived in the family with him, he never offered the most trifling abuse; on the contrary, his whole conduct towards me was strictly honorable. I mourned his loss as that of a tender brother, and shall recollect him through life with emotions of friendship and gratitude.

I lived undisturbed, without hearing a word on the subject of my land, till the great Council was held at Big Tree, in 1797, when Farmer's Brother, whose Indian name is Ho-na-ye-wus, sent for me to attend the council. When I got there, he told me that my brother had spoken to him to see that I had a piece of land reserved for my use; and that then was the time for me to receive it.—He requested that I would choose for myself and describe the bounds of a piece that would suit me. I accordingly told him the place of beginning, and then went round a tract that I judged would be sufficient for my purpose, (knowing that it would include the Gardow Flats,) by stating certain bounds with which I was acquainted.

When the Council was opened, and the business afforded a proper opportunity, Farmer's Brother presented my claim, and rehearsed the request of my brother. Red Jacket, whose Indian name is Sagu-yu-what-hah, which interpreted, is Keeper-awake, opposed me or my claim with all his influence and eloquence. Farmer's Brother insisted upon the necessity, propriety and expediency of his proposition, and got the land granted. The deed was made and signed, securing to me the title to all the land I had described; under the same restrictions and regulations that other Indian lands are subject to.

That land has ever since been known by the name of the Gardow Tract.

Red Jacket not only opposed my claim at the Council, but he withheld my money two or three years, on the account of my lands having been granted without his consent. Parrish and Jones at length convinced him that it was the white people, and not the Indians who had given me the land, and compelled him to pay over all the money which he had retained on my account.

My land derived its name, Gardow, from a hill that is within its limits, which is called in the Seneca language Kautam. Kautam when interpreted signifies up and down, or down and up, and is applied to a hill that you will ascend and descend in passing it; or to a valley. It has been said that Gardow was the name of my husband Hiokatoo, and that my land derived its name from him; that however was a mistake, for the old man always considered Gardow a nickname, and was uniformly offended when called by it.

About three hundred acres of my land, when I first saw it, was open flats, lying on the Genesee River, which it is supposed was cleared by a race of inhabitants who preceded the first Indian settlements in this part of the country. The Indians are confident that many parts of this country were settled and for a number of years occupied by people of whom their fathers never had any tradition, as they never had seen them. Whence those people originated, and whither they went, I have never heard one of our oldest and wisest Indians pretend to guess. When I first came to Genishau, the bank of

Fall Brook had just slid off and exposed a large number of human bones, which the Indians said were buried there long before their fathers ever saw the place; and that they did not know what kind of people they were. It however was and is believed by our people, that they were not Indians.

My flats were extremely fertile; but needed more labor than my daughters and myself were able to perform, to produce a sufficient quantity of grain and other necessary productions of the earth, for the consumption of our family. The land had lain uncultivated so long that it was thickly covered with weeds of almost every description. In order that we might live more easy, Mr. Parrish, with the consent of the chiefs, gave me liberty to lease or let my land to white people to till on shares. I accordingly let it out, and have continued to do so, which makes my task less burthensome, while at the same time I am more comfortably supplied with the means of support.

10

Happy situation of her Family.—Disagreement between her sons
    Thomas and John.—Her Advice to them, &c.—John kills
    Thomas.—Her Affliction.—Council. Decision of the Chiefs,
    &c.—Life of Thomas.—His Wives, Children, &c.—Cause of
    his Death, &c.

I have frequently heard it asserted by white people, and can
truly say from my own experience, that the time at which
parents take the most satisfaction and comfort with their
families is when their children are young, incapable of providing for their own wants, and are about the fireside, where
they can be daily observed and instructed.

    Few mothers, perhaps, have had less trouble with their
children during their minority than myself. In general, my
children were friendly to each other, and it was very seldom
that I knew them to have the least difference or quarrel: so
far, indeed, were they from rendering themselves or me
uncomfortable, that I considered myself happy—more so
than commonly falls to the lot of parents, especially to women.

    My happiness in this respect, however, was not without
alloy; for my son Thomas, from some cause unknown to me,
from the time he was a small lad, always called his brother
John, a witch, which was the cause, as they grew towards
manhood, of frequent and severe quarrels between them,
and gave me much trouble and anxiety for their safety. After
Thomas and John arrived to manhood, in addition to the
former charge, John got two wives, with whom he lived till

the time of his death. Although polygamy was tolerated in our tribe, Thomas considered it a violation of good and wholesome rules in society, and tending directly to destroy that friendly social intercourse and love, that ought to be the happy result of matrimony and chastity. Consequently, he frequently reprimanded John, by telling him that his conduct was beneath the dignity, and inconsistent with the principles of good Indians; indecent and unbecoming a gentleman; and, as he never could reconcile himself to it, he was frequently, almost constantly, when they were together, talking to him on the same subject. John always resented such reprimand, and reproof, with a great degree of passion, though they never quarrelled, unless Thomas was intoxicated.

In his fits of drunkenness, Thomas seemed to lose all his natural reason, and to conduct like a wild or crazy man, without regard to relatives, decency or propriety. At such times he often threatened to take my life for having raised a witch, (as he called John), and has gone so far as to raise his tomahawk to split my head. He, however, never struck me; but on John's account he struck Hiokatoo, and thereby excited in John a high degree of indignation, which was extinguished only by blood.

For a number of years their difficulties, and consequent unhappiness, continued and rather increased, continually exciting in my breast the most fearful apprehensions, and greatest anxiety for their safety. With tears in my eyes, I advised them to become reconciled to each other, and to be friendly; told them the consequences of their continuing to cherish so much malignity and malice, that it would end in their destruction, the disgrace of their families, and bring me down to the grave. No one can conceive of the constant trouble that I daily endured on their accounts—on the account of my two oldest sons, whom I loved equally, and with all the feelings and affection of a tender mother, stimulated by an anxious concern for their fate. Parents, mothers especially, will love their children, though ever so unkind and disobedient. Their eyes of compassion, of real sentimental affection, will be involuntarily extended after them, in their greatest excesses of iniquity; and those fine filaments of consanguinity, which gently entwine themselves around the heart where filial love and parental care is equal, will be lengthened, and enlarged to cords seemingly of sufficient strength to reach and reclaim the wanderer. I know that such exercises are frequently unavailing; but, notwithstanding their ultimate failure, it still remains true, and ever will, that the love of a parent for a disobedient child, will increase, and grow more and more ardent, so long as a hope of its reformation is capable of stimulating a disappointed breast.

My advice and expostulations with my sons were abortive; and year after year their disaffection for each other increased. At length, Thomas came to my house on the 1st day of July, 1811, in my absence, somewhat intoxicated, where he found John, with whom he immediately commenced a quarrel on their old subjects of difference.—John's anger became desperate. He caught Thomas by the hair of his head, dragged him out at the door and there killed him, by a blow which he gave him on the head with his tomahawk!

I returned soon after, and found my son lifeless at the door, on the spot where he was killed! No one can judge of my feelings on seeing this mournful spectacle; and what greatly added to my distress, was the fact that he had fallen by the murderous hand of his brother! I felt my situation unsupportable. Having passed through various scenes of trouble of the most cruel and trying kind, I had hoped to spend my few remaining days in quietude, and to die in peace, surrounded by my family. This fatal event, however, seemed to be a stream of woe poured into my cup of afflictions, filling it even to overflowing, and blasting all my prospects.

As soon as I had recovered a little from the shock which I felt at the sight of my departed son, and some of my neighbors had come in to assist in taking care of the corpse, I hired Shanks, an Indian, to go to Buffalo, and carry the sorrowful news of Thomas' death, to our friends at that place, and request the Chiefs to hold a Council, and dispose of John as they should think proper. Shanks set out on his errand immediately, and John, fearing that he should be apprehended and punished for the crime he had committed, at the same time went off towards Caneadea.

Thomas was decently interred in a style corresponding with his rank.

The Chiefs soon assembled in council on the trial of John, and after having seriously examined the matter according to their laws, justified his conduct, and acquitted him. They considered Thomas to have been the first transgressor, and that for the abuses which he had offered, he had merited from John the treatment that he had received.

John, on learning the decision of the council, returned to his family.

Thomas (except when intoxicated, which was not frequent,) was a kind and tender child, willing to assist me in my labor, and to remove every obstacle to my comfort. His natural abilities were said to be of a superior cast, and he soared above the trifling subjects of revenge, which are common amongst Indians, as being far beneath his attention. In his childish and boyish days, his natural turn was to practice in the art of war, though he despised the cruelties that the warriors inflicted upon their subjugated enemies. He was manly in his deportment, courageous and active; and commanded respect. Though he appeared well pleased with peace, he was cunning in Indian warfare, and succeeded to admiration in the execution of his plans.

At the age of fourteen or fifteen years, he went into the war with manly fortitude, armed with a tomahawk and scalping knife; and when he returned, brought one white man a prisoner, whom he had taken with his own hands, on the west branch of the Susquehannah river. It so happened, that as he was looking out for his enemies, he discovered two men boiling sap in the woods. He watched them unperceived, till dark when he advanced with a noiseless step to where they were standing, caught one of them before they were apprized of danger, and conducted him to the camp. He was well treated while a prisoner, and redeemed at the close of the war.

At the time Kaujisestaugeau gave me my liberty to go to my friends, Thomas was anxious to go with me; but as I have before observed, the Chiefs would not suffer him to leave them on the account of his courage and skill in war: expecting that they should need his assistance. He was a great Counsellor and a Chief when quite young; and in the last capacity, went two or three times to Philadelphia to assist in making treaties with the people of the states.

Thomas had four wives, by whom he had eight children. Jacob Jemison, his second son by his last wife, who is at this time twenty-seven or twenty-eight years of age, went to Dartmouth college, in the spring of 1816, for the purpose of receiving a good education, where it was said that he was an industrious scholar, and made great proficiency in the study of the different branches to which he attended. Having spent two years at that Institution, he returned in the winter of 1818, and is now at Buffalo; where I have understood that he contemplates commencing the study of medicine, as a profession.

Thomas, at the time he was killed, was a few moons over fifty-two years old, and John was forty-eight. As he was naturally good natured, and possessed a friendly disposition, he would not have come to so untimely an end, had it not been for his intemperance. He fell a victim to the use of ardent spirits—a poison that will soon exterminate the Indian tribes in this part of the country, and leave their names without a root or branch. The thought is melancholy; but no arguments, no examples, however persuasive or impressive, are sufficient to deter an Indian for an hour from taking the potent draught, which he knows at the time will derange his faculties, reduce him to a level with the beasts, or deprive him of life!

11

Death of Hiokatoo.—Biography.—His Birth.—Education.—Goes against the Cherokees, &c.—Bloody Battle, &c.—His success and cruelties in the French War.—Battle at Fort Freeland.—Capts. Dougherty and Boon killed.—His Cruelties in the neighborhood of Cherry Valley, &c.—Indians remove their general Encampment.—In 1782, Col. Crawford is sent to destroy them, &c.—Is met by a Traitor,—Battle.—Crawford's Men surprized.—Irregular Retreat.—Crawford and Doct. Night taken.—Council.—Crawford Condemned and Burnt.—Aggravating Circumstances.—Night is sentenced to be Burnt.—Is Painted by Hiokatoo.—Is conducted off, &c.—His fortunate escape.—Hiokatoo in the French War takes Col. Canton.—His Sentence.—Is bound on a wild Colt that runs loose three days.—Returns Alive.—Is made to run the Gauntlet.—Gets knocked down, &c.—Is Redeemed and sent Home.—Hiokatoo's enmity to the Cherokees, &c.—His Height.—Strength—Speed, &c.

IN the month of November 1811, my husband Hiokatoo, who had been sick four years of the consumption, died at the advanced age of one hundred and three years, as nearly as the time could be estimated. He was the last that remained to me of our family connection, or rather of my old friends with whom I was adopted, except a part of one family, which now lives at Tonewanta.

Hiokatoo was buried decently, and had all the insignia of a veteran warrior buried with him; consisting of a war club,

128

tomahawk and scalping knife, a powder-flask, flint, a piece
of spunk, a small cake and a cup; and in his best clothing.

Hiokatoo was an old man when I first saw him; but he was
by no means enervated. During the term of nearly fifty years
that I lived with him, I received, according to Indian customs,
all the kindness and attention that was my due as his wife.—
Although war was his trade from his youth till old age and
decrepitude stopt his career, he uniformly treated me with
tenderness, and never offered an insult.

I have frequently heard him repeat the history of his life
from his childhood; and when he came to that part which
related to his actions, his bravery and his valor in war; when
he spoke of the ambush, the combat, the spoiling of his enemies and the sacrifice of the victims, his nerves seemed strung
with youthful ardor, the warmth of the able warrior seemed
to animate his frame, and to produce the heated gestures
which he had practiced in middle age. He was a man of tender
feelings to his friends, ready and willing to assist them in
distress, yet, as a warrior, his cruelties to his enemies perhaps
were unparalleled, and will not admit a word of palliation.

Hiokatoo, was born in one of the tribes of the Six Nations
that inhabited the banks of the Susquehannah; or, rather he
belonged to a tribe of the Senecas that made, at the time of
the great Indian treaty, a part of those nations. He was own
cousin to Farmer's Brother, a Chief who had been justly
celebrated for his worth. Their mothers were sisters, and it
was through the influence of Farmer's Brother, that I became
Hiokatoo's wife.

In early life, Hiokatoo showed signs of thirst for blood,
by attending only to the art of war, in the use of the tomahawk
and scalping knife; and in practising cruelties upon every
thing that chanced to fall into his hands, which was susceptible
of pain. In that way he learned to use his implements of
war effectually, and at the same time blunted all those fine
feelings and tender sympathies that are naturally excited, by
hearing or seeing, a fellow being in distress. He could inflict
the most excruciating tortures upon his enemies, and prided
himself upon his fortitude, in having performed the most
barbarous ceremonies and tortures, without the least degree
of pity or remorse. Thus qualified, when very young he was

initiated into scenes of carnage, by being engaged in the wars that prevailed amongst the Indian tribes.

In the year 1731, he was appointed a runner, to assist in collecting an army to go against the Cotawpes, Cherokees and other southern Indians. A large army was collected, and after a long and fatiguing march, met its enemies in what was then called the "low, dark and bloody lands," near the mouth of Red River, in what is now called the state of Kentucky.* The Cotawpes† and their associates, had, by some means, been apprized of their approach, and lay in ambush to take them at once, when they should come within their reach, and destroy the whole army. The northern Indians, with their usual sagacity, discovered the situation of their enemies, rushed upon the ambuscade and massacred 1200 on the spot. The battle continued for two days and two nights, with the utmost severity, in which the northern Indians were victorious, and so far succeeded in destroying the Cotawpes that they at that time ceased to be a nation. The victors suffered an immense loss in killed; but gained the hunting ground, which was their grand object, though the Cherokees would not give it up in a treaty, or consent to make peace. Bows and arrows, at that time, were in general use, though a few guns were employed.

From that time he was engaged in a number of battles in which Indians only were engaged, and made fighting his business, till the commencement of the French war. In those battles he took a number of Indians prisoners, whom he killed by tying them to trees and then setting small Indian boys to shooting at them with arrows, till death finished the misery of the sufferers; a process that frequently took two days for its completion!

During the French war he was in every battle that was fought on the Susquehannah and Ohio rivers; and was so fortunate as never to have been taken prisoner.

* Those powerful armies met near the place that is now called Clarksville, which is situated at the fork where Red River joins the Cumberland, a few miles above the line between Kentucky and Tennessee.
† The Author acknowledges himself unacquainted, from Indian history, with a nation of this name; but as 90 years have elapsed since the date of this occurrence, it is highly probable that such a nation did exist, and that it was absolutely exterminated at that eventful period.

At Braddock's defeat he took two white prisoners, and burnt them alive in a fire of his own kindling.

In 1777, he was in the battle at Fort Freeland, in Northumberland county, Penn. The fort contained a great number of women and children, and was defended only by a small garrison. The force that went against it consisted of 100 British regulars, commanded by a Col. McDonald, and 300 Indians under Hiokatoo. After a short but bloody engagement, the fort was surrendered; the women and children were sent under an escort to the next fort below, and the men and boys taken off by a party of British to the general Indian encampment. As soon as the fort had capitulated and the firing had ceased, Hiokatoo with the help of a few Indians tomahawked every wounded American while earnestly begging with uplifted hands for quarters.

The massacre was but just finished when Capts. Dougherty and Boon arrived with a reinforcement to assist the garrison. On their arriving in sight of the fort they saw that it had surrendered, and that an Indian was holding the flag. This so much inflamed Capt. Dougherty that he left his command, stept forward and shot the Indian at the first fire. Another took the flag, and had no sooner got it erected than Dougherty dropt him as he had the first. A third presumed to hold it, who was also shot down by Dougherty. Hiokatoo, exasperated at the sight of such bravery, sallied out with a party of his Indians, and killed Capts. Dougherty, Boon, and fourteen men, at the first fire. The remainder of the two companies escaped by taking to flight, and soon arrived at the fort which they had left but a few hours before.

In an expedition that went out against Cherry Valley and the neighboring settlements, Captain David, a Mohawk Indian, was first, and Hiokatoo the second in command. The force consisted of several hundred Indians, who were determined on mischief, and the destruction of the whites. A continued series of wantonness and barbarity characterized their career, for they plundered and burnt every thing that came in their way, and killed a number of persons, among whom were several infants, whom Hiokatoo butchered or dashed upon the stones with his own hands. Besides the instances which have been mentioned, he was in a number of parties

during the revolutionary war, where he ever acted a conspicu-
ous part.

The Indians having removed the seat of their depredations and war to the frontiers of Pennsylvania, Ohio, Kentucky and the neighboring territories, assembled a large force
at Upper Sandusky, their place of general rendezvous, from
whence they went out to the various places which they designed to sacrifice.

Tired of the desolating scenes that were so often witnessed, and feeling a confidence that the savages might be
subdued, and an end put to their crimes, the American government raised a regiment, consisting of 300 volunteers, for
the purpose of dislodging them from their cantonment and
preventing further barbarities. Col. William Crawford and
Lieut. Col. David Williamson, men who had been thoroughly
tried and approved, were commissioned by Gen. Washington
to take the command of a service that seemed all-important
to the welfare of the country. In the month of July, 1782,
well armed and provided with a sufficient quantity of provision, this regiment made an expeditious march through the
wilderness to Upper Sandusky, where, as had been anticipated, they found the Indians assembled in full force at their
encampment, prepared to receive an attack.

As Col. Crawford and his brave band advanced, and
when they had got within a short distance from the town,
they were met by a white man, with a flag of truce from the
Indians, who proposed to Col. Crawford that if he would
surrender himself and his men to the Indians, their lives
should be spared; but, that if they persisted in their undertaking, and attacked the town, they should all be massacred to
a man.

Crawford, while hearing the proposition, attentively sur-
veyed its bearer, and recognized in his features one of his
former schoolmates and companions, with whom he was perfectly acquainted, by the name of Simon Gurty. Gurty, but
a short time before this, had been a soldier in the American
army, in the same regiment with Crawford; but on the account
of his not having received the promotion that he expected,
he became disaffected—swore an eternal war with his countrymen, fled to the Indians, and joined them, as a leader well
qualified to conduct them to where they could satiate their

thirst for blood, upon the innocent, unoffending and defense-less settlers.

Crawford sternly inquired of the traitor if his name was not Simon Gurty; and being answered in the affirmative, he informed him that he despised the offer which he had made; and that he should not surrender his army unless he should be compelled to do so, by a superior force.

Gurty returned, and Crawford immediately commenced an engagement that lasted till night, without the appearance of victory on either side, when the firing ceased, and the combatants on both sides retired to take refreshment, and to rest through the night. Crawford encamped in the woods near half a mile from the town, where, after the centinels were placed, and each had taken his ration, they slept on their arms, that they might be instantly ready in case they should be attacked. The stillness of death hovered over the little army, and sleep relieved the whole, except the wakeful centi-nels who vigilantly attended to their duty.—But what was their surprise, when they found late in the night, that they were surrounded by the Indians on every side, except a narrow space between them and the town? Every man was under arms, and the officers instantly consulted each other on the best method of escaping; for they saw that to fight, would be useless, and that to surrender, would be death.

Crawford proposed to retreat through the ranks of the enemy in an opposite direction from the town, as being the most sure course to take. Lt. Col. Williamson advised to march directly through the town, where there appeared to be no Indians, and the fires were yet burning.

There was no time or place for debates: Col. Crawford, with sixty followers retreated on the route that he had pro-posed by attempting to rush through the enemy; but they had no sooner got amongst the Indians, than every man was killed or taken prisoner! Amongst the prisoners, were Col. Crawford, and Doct. Night, surgeon of the regiment.

Lt. Col. Williamson, with the remainder of the regiment, together with the wounded, set out at the same time that Crawford did, went through the town without losing a man, and by the help of good guides arrived at their homes in safety.

The next day after the engagement the Indians disposed

of all their prisoners to the different tribes, except Col. Crawford and Doct. Night; but those unfortunate men were reserved for a more cruel destiny. A council was immediately held on Sandusky plains, consisting of all the Chiefs and warriors, ranged in their customary order, in a circular form; and Crawford and Night were brought forward and seated in the centre of the circle.

The council being opened, the Chiefs began to examine Crawford on various subjects relative to the war. At length they enquired who conducted the military operations of the American army on the Ohio and Susquehannah rivers, during the year before; and who had led that army against them with so much skill, and so uniform success? Crawford very honestly and without suspecting any harm from his reply, promptly answered that he was the man who had led his countrymen to victory, who had driven the enemy from the settlements, and by that means had procured a great degree of happiness to many of his fellow-citizens. Upon hearing this, a Chief, who had lost a son in the year before, in a battle where Colonel Crawford commanded, left his station in the council, stepped to Crawford, blacked his face, and at the same time told him that the next day he should be burnt.

The council was immediately dissolved on its hearing the sentence from the Chief, and the prisoners were taken off the ground, and kept in custody through the night. Crawford now viewed his fate as sealed; and despairing of ever returning to his home or his country, only dreaded the tediousness of death, as commonly inflicted by the savages, and earnestly hoped that he might be despatched at a single blow.

Early the next morning, the Indians assembled at the place of execution, and Crawford was led to the post—the goal of savage torture, to which he was fastened. The post was a stick of timber placed firmly in the ground, having an arm framed in at the top, and extending some six or eight feet from it, like the arm of a sign post. A pile of wood containing about two cords, lay a few feet from the place where he stood, which he was informed was to be kindled into a fire that would burn him alive, as many had been burnt on the same spot, who had been much less deserving than himself.

Gurty stood and composedly looked on the preparations

that were making for the funeral of one his former playmates; a hero by whose side he had fought; of a man whose valor had won laurels which, if he could have returned, would have been strewed upon his grave, by his grateful countrymen. Dreading the agony that he saw he was about to feel, Craw ford used every argument which his perilous situation could suggest to prevail upon Gurty to ransom him at any price, and deliver him (as it was in his power,) from the savages, and their torments. Gurty heard his prayers, and expostulations, and saw his tears with indifference, and finally told the forsaken victim that he would not procure him a moment's respite, nor afford him the most trifling assistance.

The Col. was then bound, stripped naked and tied by his wrists to the arm, which extended horizontally from the post, in such a manner that his arms were extended over his head, with his feet just standing upon the ground. This being done the savages placed the wood in a circle around him at the distance of a few feet, in order that his misery might be protracted to the greatest length, and then kindled it in a number of places at the same time. The flames arose and the scorching heat became almost insupportable. Again he prayed to Gurty in all the anguish of his torment, to rescue him from the fire, or shoot him dead upon the spot. A demoniac smile suffused the countenance of Gurty, while he calmly replied to the dying suppliant, that he had no pity for his sufferings; but that he was then satisfying that spirit of revenge, which for a long time he had hoped to have an opportunity to wreak upon him. Nature now almost exhausted from the intensity of the heat, he settled down a little, when a squaw threw coals of fire and embers upon him, which made him groan most piteously, while the whole camp rung with exultation. During the execution they manifested all the exstacy of a complete triumph. Poor Crawford soon died and was entirely consumed.

Thus ended the life of a patriot and hero, who had been an intimate with Gen. Washington, and who shared in an eminent degree the confidence of that great, good man, to whom, in the time of revolutionary perils, the sons of legitimate freedom looked with a degree of faith in his mental resources, unequalled in the history of the world.

That tragedy being ended, Doct. Night was informed that on the next day he should be burnt in the same manner that his comrade Crawford had been, at Lower Sandusky. Hiokatoo, who had been a leading chief in the battle with, and in the execution of Crawford, painted Doct. Night's face black, and then bound and gave him up to two able bodied Indians to conduct to the place of execution.

They set off with him immediately, and travelled till towards evening, when they halted to encamp till morning. The afternoon had been very rainy, and the storm still continued, which rendered it very difficult for the Indians to kindle a fire. Night observing the difficulty under which they labored, made them to understand by signs, that if they would unbind him, he would assist them.—They accordingly unloosed him, and he soon succeeded in making a fire by the application of small dry stuff which he was at considerable trouble to procure. While the Indians were warming themselves, the Doct. continued to gather wood to last through the night, and in doing this, he found a club which he placed in a situation from whence he could take it conveniently whenever an opportunity should present itself, in which he could use it effectually. The Indians continued warming, till at length the Doct. saw that they had placed themselves in a favorable position for the execution of his design, when, stimulated by the love of life, he cautiously took his club and at two blows knocked them both down. Determined to finish the work of death which he had so well begun, he drew one of their scalping knives, with which he beheaded and scalped them both! He then took a rifle, tomahawk, and some ammunition, and directed his course for home, where he arrived without having experienced any difficulty on his journey.

The next morning, the Indians took the track of their victim and his attendants, to go to Lower Sandusky, and there execute the sentence which they had pronounced upon him. But what was their surprise and disappointment, when they arrived at the place of encampment, where they found their trusty friends scalped and decapitated, and that their prisoner had made his escape?—Chagrined beyond measure, they immediately separated, and went in every direction in pursuit of their prey; but after having spent a number of days unsuccessfully, they gave up the chase, and returned to their encampment.*

In the time of the French war, in an engagement that took place on the Ohio river, Hiokatoo took a British Col. by the name of Simon Canton, whom he carried to the Indian encampment. A council was held, and the Col. was sentenced to suffer death, by being tied on a wild colt, with his face towards its tail, and then having the colt turned loose to run where it pleased. He was accordingly tied on, and the colt let loose, agreeable to the sentence. The colt run two days and then returned with its rider yet alive. The Indians, thinking that he would never die in that way, took him off, and made him run the gauntlet three times; but in the last race a squaw knocked him down, and he was supposed to have been dead. He, however, recovered, and was sold for fifty dollars to a Frenchman, who sent him as a prisoner to Detroit. On the return of the Frenchman to Detroit, the Col. besought him to ransom him, and give, or set him at liberty, with so much warmth, and promised with so much solemnity, to reward him as one of the best of benefactors, if he would let him go, that the Frenchman took his word, and sent him home to his family. The Col. remembered his promise, and in a short time sent his deliverer one hundred and fifty dollars, as a reward for his generosity.

Since the commencement of the revolutionary war, Hiokatoo has been in seventeen campaigns, four of which were in the Cherokee war. He was so great an enemy to the Chero-

* I have understood, (from unauthenticated sources however,) that soon after the revolutionary war, Doct. Night published a pamphlet, containing an account of the battle at Sandusky, and of his own sufferings. My information on this subject, was derived from a different quarter.

The subject of this narrative in giving the account of her last husband, Hiokatoo, referred us to Mr. George Jemison, who, (as it will be noticed) lived on her land a number of years, and who had frequently heard the old Chief relate the story of his life; particularly that part which related to his military career. Mr. Jemison, on being enquired of, gave the foregoing account, partly from his own personal knowledge, and the remainder, from the account given by Hiokatoo.

Mr. Jemison was in the battle, was personally acquainted with Col. Crawford, and one that escaped with Lt. Col. Williamson. We have no doubt of the truth of the statement, and have therefore inserted the whole account, as an addition to the historical facts which are daily coming into a state of preservation, in relation to the American Revolution.

kees, and so fully determined upon their subjugation, that on his march to their country, he raised his own army for those four campaigns, and commanded it; and also superintended its subsistence. In one of those campaigns, which continued two whole years without intermission, he attacked his enemies on the Mobile, drove them to the country of the Creek Nation, where he continued to harass them, till being tired of war, he returned to his family. He brought home a great number of scalps, which he had taken from the enemy, and ever seemed to possess an unconquerable will that the Cherokees might be utterly destroyed. Towards the close of his last fighting in that country, he took two squaws, whom he sold on his way home for money to defray the expense of his journey.

Hiokatoo was about six feet four or five inches high, large boned, and rather inclined to leanness. He was very stout and active, for a man of his size, for it was said by himself and others, that he had never found an Indian who could keep up with him on a race, or throw him at wrestling. His eye was quick and penetrating; and his voice was of that harsh and powerful kind, which, amongst Indians, always commands attention. His health had been uniformly good. He never was confined by sickness, till he was attacked with the consumption, four years before his death. And, although he had, from his earliest days, been inured to almost constant fatigue, and exposure to the inclemency of the weather, in the open air, he seemed to lose the vigor of the prime of life only by the natural decay occasioned by old age.

12

Her Troubles Renewed.—John's Jealousy towards his brother Jesse.—Circumstances attending the Murder of Jesse Jemison.—Her Grief.—His Funeral—Age—Filial Kindness, &c.

BEING now left a widow in my old age, to mourn the loss of a husband, who had treated me well, and with whom I had raised five children, and having suffered the loss of an affectionate son, I fondly fostered the hope that my melancholy vicissitudes had ended, and that the remainder of my time would be characterized by nothing unpropitious. My children, dutiful and kind, lived near me, and apparently nothing obstructed our happiness.

But a short time, however, elapsed after my husband's death, before my troubles were renewed with redoubled severity.

John's hands having been once stained in the blood of a brother, it was not strange that after his acquittal, every person of his acquaintance should shun him, from a fear of his repeating upon them the same ceremony that he had practiced upon Thomas. My son Jesse, went to Mt. Morris, a few miles from home, on business, in the winter after the death of his father; and it so happened that his brother John was there, who requested Jesse to come home with him. Jesse, fearing that John would commence a quarrel with him on the way, declined the invitation, and tarried over night.

From that time John conceived himself despised by Jesse, and was highly enraged at the treatment which he had received. Very little was said, however, and it all passed off, apparently, till sometime in the month of May, 1812, at which time Mr. Robert Whaley, who lived in the town of Castile, within four miles of me, came to my house early on Monday morning, to hire George Chongo, my son-in-law, and John and Jesse, to go that day and help him slide a quantity of boards from the top of the hill to the river, where he calculated to build a raft of them for market.

They all concluded to go with Mr. Whaley, and made ready as soon as possible. But before they set out I charged them not to drink any whiskey: for I was confident that if they did, they would surely have a quarrel in consequence of it. They went and worked till almost night, when a quarrel ensued between Chongo and Jesse, in consequence of the whiskey that they had drank through the day, which terminated in a battle, and Chongo got whipped.

When Jesse had got through with Chongo, he told Mr. Whaley that he would go home, and directly went off. He, however, went but a few rods before he stopped and lay down by the side of a log to wait, (as was supposed,) for company. John, as soon as Jesse was gone, went to Mr. Whaley, with his knife in his hand, and bade him jogo; (i.e. be gone,) at the same time telling him that Jesse was a bad man. Mr. Whaley, seeing that his countenance was changed, and that he was determined upon something desperate, was alarmed for his own safety, and turned towards home, leaving Chongo on the ground drunk, near to where Jesse had lain, who by this time had got up, and was advancing towards John. Mr. Whaley was soon out of hearing of them; but some of his workmen staid till it was dark. Jesse came up to John, and said to him, you want more whiskey, and more fighting, and after a few words, went at him, to try in the first place to get away his knife. In this he did not succeed, and they parted. By this time the night had come on, and it was dark. Again they clenched and at length in their struggle they both fell. John, having his knife in his hand, came under, and in that situation gave Jesse a fatal stab with his knife, and repeated the blows till Jesse cried out, brother, you have killed me, quit his hold and settled back upon the ground.—Upon hearing this, John left him and came to Thomas' widow's house, told them that he had been fighting with their uncle, whom he had killed, and showed them his knife.

Next morning as soon as it was light, Thomas' and John's children came and told me that Jesse was dead in the woods, and also informed me how he came by his death. John soon followed them and informed me himself of all that had taken place between him and his brother, and seemed to be somewhat sorrowful for his conduct. You can better imagine what my feelings were than I can describe them. My darling son, my youngest child, him on whom I depended, was dead; and I in my old age left destitute of a helping hand!

As soon as it was consistent for me, I got Mr. George Jemison (of whom I shall have occasion to speak,) to go with his sleigh to where Jesse was, and bring him home, a distance of 3 or 4 miles. My daughter Polly arrived at the fatal spot first: we got there soon after her; though I went the whole distance on foot. By this time, Chongo, (who was left on the ground drunk the night before,) had become sober and sensible of the great misfortune which had happened to our family.

I was overcome with grief at the sight of my murdered son, and so far lost the command of myself as to be almost frantic; and those who were present were obliged to hold me from going near him.

On examining the body it was found that it had received eighteen wounds so deep and large that it was believed that either of them would have proved mortal. The corpse was carried to my house, and kept till the Thursday following, when it was buried after the manner of burying white people.

Jesse was twenty-seven or eight years old when he was killed. His temper had been uniformly very mild and friendly; and he was inclined to copy after the white people; both in his manners and dress. Although he was naturally temperate, he occasionally became intoxicated; but never was quarrelsome or mischievous. With the white people he was intimate, and learned from them their habits of industry, which he was fond of practising, especially when my comfort demanded his labor. As I have observed, it is the custom amongst the Indians, for the women to perform all the labor in, and out of doors, and I had the whole to do, with the help of my daughters, till Jesse arrived to a sufficient age to assist us. He was disposed to labor in the cornfield, to chop my wood, milk my cows, and attend to any kind of business that would make my task the lighter. On the account of his having been my youngest child, and so willing to help me, I am sensible that I loved him better than I did either of my other children. After he began to understand my situation, and the means of rendering it more easy, I never wanted for any thing that was in his power to bestow; but since his death, as I have had all my labor to perform alone, I have constantly seen hard times.

Jesse shunned the company of his brothers, and the Indians generally, and never attended their frolics; and it was supposed that this, together with my partiality for him, were the causes which excited in John so great a degree of envy, that nothing short of death would satisfy it.

13

Mrs. Jemison is informed that she has a Cousin in the Neighborhood, by the name of George Jemison.—His Poverty.—Her Kindness.—His Ingratitude.—Her Trouble from Land Speculation.—Her Cousin moves off.

A year or two before the death of my husband, Capt. H. Jones sent me word, that a cousin of mine was then living in Leicester, (a few miles from Gardow,) by the name of George Jemison, and as he was very poor, thought it advisable for me to go and see him, and take him home to live with me on my land. My Indian friends were pleased to hear that one of my relatives was so near, and also advised me to send for him and his family immediately. I accordingly had him and his family moved into one of my houses, in the month of March, 1810.

He said that he was my father's brother's son—that his father did not leave Europe, till after the French War in America, and that when he did come over, he settled in Pennsylvania, where he died. George had no personal knowledge of my father; but from information, was confident that the relationship which he claimed between himself and me, actually existed. Although I had never before heard of my father having had but one brother, (him who was killed at Fort Necessity,) yet I knew that he might have had others, and, as the story of George carried with it a probability that it was true, I received him as a kinsman, and treated

143

him with every degree of friendship which his situation demanded.*

I found that he was destitute of the means of subsistence, and in debt to the amount of seventy dollars, without the ability to pay one cent. He had no cow, and finally, was completely poor. I paid his debts to the amount of seventy-two dollars, and bought him a cow, for which I paid twenty dollars, and a sow and pigs, that I paid eight dollars for. I also paid sixteen dollars for pork that I gave him, and furnished him with other provisions and furniture; so that his family was comfortable. As he was destitute of a team, I furnished him with one, and also supplied him with tools for farming. In addition to all this, I let him have one of Thomas' cows, for two seasons.

My only object in mentioning his poverty, and the articles with which I supplied him, is to show how ungrateful a person can be for favors, and how soon a kind benefactor will, to all appearance, be forgotten.

Thus furnished with the necessary implements of husbandry, a good team, and as much land as he could till, he commenced farming on my flats, and for some time labored well. At length, however, he got an idea that if he could become the owner of a part of my reservation, he could live more easy, and certainly be more rich, and accordingly set himself about laying a plan to obtain it, in the easiest manner possible.

I supported Jemison and his family eight years, and probably should have continued to have done so to this day, had it not been for the occurrence of the following circumstance.

When he had lived with me some six or seven years, a friend of mine told me that as Jemison was my cousin, and very poor, I ought to give him a piece of land that he might have something whereon to live, that he would call his own. My friend and Jemison were then together at my house, prepared to complete a bargain. I asked how much land he wanted? Jemison said that he should be glad to receive his

---

* Mrs. Jemison is now confident that George Jemison is not her cousin, and thinks that he claimed the relationship, only to gain assistance: But the old gentleman, who is now living, is certain that his and her father were brothers, as before stated.

old field (as he called it) containing about fourteen acres, and a new one that contained twenty-six.

I observed to them that as I was incapable of transacting business of that nature, I would wait till Mr. Thomas Clute, (a neighbor on whom I depended,) should return from Albany, before I should do any thing about it. To this Jemison replied that if I waited till Mr. Clute returned, he should not get the land at all, and appeared very anxious to have the business closed without delay. On my part, I felt disposed to give him some land, but knowing my ignorance of writing, feared to do it alone, lest they might include as much land as they pleased, without my knowledge.

They then read the deed which my friends had prepared before he came from home, describing a piece of land by certain bounds that were a specified number of chains and links from each other. Not understanding the length of a chain or link, I described the bounds of a piece of land that I intended Jemison should have, which they said was just the same that the deed contained and no more. I told them that the deed must not include a lot that was called the Steele place, and they assured me that it did not. Upon this, putting confidence in them both, I signed the deed to George Jemison, containing, and conveying to him as I supposed, forty acres of land. The deed being completed they charged me never to mention the bargain which I had then made to any person; because if I did, they said it would spoil the contract. The whole matter was afterwards disclosed; when it was found that that deed instead of containing only forty acres, contained four hundred, and that one half of it actually belonged to my friend, as it had been given to him by Jemison as a reward for his trouble in procuring the deed, in the fraudulent manner above mentioned.

My friend, however, by the advice of some well disposed people, awhile afterwards gave up his claim, but Jemison held his till he sold it for a trifle to a gentleman in the south part of Genesee county.

Sometime after the death of my son Thomas, one of his sons went to Jemison to get the cow that I had let him have two years; but Jemison refused to let her go, and struck the boy so violent a blow as to almost kill him. Jemison then ran to Jellis Clute, Esq. to procure a warrant to take the boy; but Young King, an Indian Chief, went down to Squawky hill to Esq. Clute's, and settled the affair by Jemison's agreeing never to use that club again. Having satisfactorily found out the friendly disposition of my cousin towards me, I got him off my premises as soon as possible.

14

Another Family Affliction.—Her son John's Occupation.—He goes to Buffalo.—Returns.—Great Slide by him considered Ominous—Trouble, &c.—He goes to Squawky Hill—Quarrels—Is murdered by two Indians.—His Funeral—Mourners, &c.—His Disposition.—Ominous Dream.—Black Chief's Advice, &c.—His Widows and Family.—His Age.—His Murderers flee.—Her Advice to them.—They set out to leave their Country.—Their Uncle's Speech to them on parting.—They return.—Jack proposes to Doctor to kill each other.—Doctor's Speech in Reply.—Jack's Suicide.—Doctor's Death.

TROUBLE seldom comes single. While George Jemison was busily engaged in his pursuit of wealth at my expense, another event of a much more serious nature occurred, which added greatly to my afflictions, and consequently destroyed, at least a part of the happiness that I had anticipated was laid up in the archives of Providence, to be dispensed on my old age.

My son John, was a doctor, considerably celebrated amongst the Indians of various tribes, for his skill in curing their diseases, by the administration of roots and herbs, which he gathered in the forests, and other places where they had been planted by the hand of nature.

In the month of April, or first of May, 1817, he was called upon to go to Buffalo, Cattaraugus and Allegany, to cure some who were sick. He went, and was absent about two months. When he returned, he observed the Great Slide of the bank of Genesee river, a short distance above my house, which had taken place during his absence; and conceiving that circumstance to be ominous of his own death, called at his sister Nancy's, told her that he should live but a few days, and wept bitterly at the near approach of his dissolution. Nancy endeavored to persuade him that his trouble was imaginary, and that he ought not to be affected by a fancy which was visionary. Her arguments were ineffectual, and afforded no alleviation to his mental sufferings. From his sister's, he went to his own house, where he stayed only two nights, and then went to Squawky Hill to procure money, with which to purchase flour for the use of his family.

While at Squawky Hill he got into the company of two Squawky Hill Indians, whose names were Doctor and Jack, with whom he drank freely, and in the afternoon had a desperate quarrel, in which his opponents, (as it was afterwards understood,) agreed to kill him. The quarrel ended, and each appeared to be friendly. John bought some spirits, of which they all drank, and then set out for home. John and an Allegany Indian were on horseback, and Doctor and Jack were on foot. It was dark when they set out. They had not proceeded far, when Doctor and Jack commenced another quarrel with John, clenched and dragged him off his horse, and then with a stone gave him so severe a blow on his head, that some of his brains were discharged from the wound. The Allegany Indian, fearing that his turn would come next, fled for safety as fast as possible.

John recovered a little from the shock he had received, and endeavored to get to an old hut that stood near; but they caught him, and with an axe cut his throat, and beat out his brains, so that when he was found the contents of his skull were lying on his arms.

Some squaws, who heard the uproar, ran to find out the cause of it; but before they had time to offer their assistance, the murders drove them into a house, and threatened to take their lives if they did not stay there, or if they made any noise.

Next morning, Esq. Clute sent me word that John was dead, and also informed me of the means by which his life was taken. A number of people went from Gardow to where the body lay, and Doct. Levi Brundridge brought it up home, where the funeral was attended after the manner of the white people. Mr. Benjamin Luther, and Mr. William Wiles, preached a sermon, and performed the funeral services; and myself and family followed the corpse to the grave as mourners. I had now buried my three sons, who had been snatched from me by the hands of violence, when I least expected it.

Although John had taken the life of his two brothers, and caused me unspeakable trouble and grief, his death made a solemn impression upon my mind, and seemed, in addition to my former misfortunes, enough to bring down my grey hairs with sorrow to the grave. Yet, on a second thought, I could not mourn for him as I had for my other sons, because I knew that his death was just, and what he had deserved for a long time, from the hand of justice.

John's vices were so great and so aggravated, that I have nothing to say in his favor: yet, as a mother, I pitied him while he lived, and have ever felt a great degree of sorrow for him, because of his bad conduct.

From his childhood, he carried something in his features indicative of an evil disposition, that would result in the perpetration of enormities of some kind; and it was the opinion and saying of Ebenezer Allen, that he would be a bad man, and be guilty of some crime deserving of death. There is no doubt but what the thoughts of murder rankled in his breast, and disturbed his mind even in his sleep; for he dreamed that he had killed Thomas for a trifling offense, and thereby forfeited his own life. Alarmed at the revelation, and fearing that he might in some unguarded moment destroy his brother, he went to the Black Chief, to whom he told the dream, and expressed his fears that the vision would be verified. Having related the dream, together with his feelings on the subject, he asked for the best advice that his old friend was capable of giving, to prevent so sad an event. The Black Chief, with his usual promptitude, told him, that from the nature of the dream, he was fearful that something serious would take place between him and Thomas; and advised him by all means to govern his temper, and avoid any quarrel which in future he might see arising, especially if Thomas was a party. John, however, did not keep the good counsel of the Chief; for soon after he killed Thomas, as I have related.

John left two wives with whom he had lived at the same time, and raised nine children. His widows are now living at Caneadea with their father, and keep their children with, and near them. His children are tolerably white, and have got light colored hair. John died about the last day of June, 1817, aged 54 years.

Doctor and Jack, having finished their murderous design, fled before they could be apprehended, and lay six weeks in the woods back of Canisteo. They then returned and sent me some wampum by Chongo (my son-in-law), and Sun-ge-waw (that is Big Kettle) expecting that I would pardon them, and suffer them to live as they had done with their tribe. I however, would not accept their wampum, but returned it with a request, that rather than have them killed, they would run away and keep out of danger.

On their receiving back the wampum, they took my advice, and prepared to leave their country and people immediately. Their relatives accompanied them a short distance on their journey, and when about to part, their old uncle, the Tall Chief, addressed them in the following pathetic and sentimental speech:

"Friends, hear my voice!—When the Great Spirit made Indians, he made them all good, and gave them good cornfields; good rivers, well stored with fish; good forests, filled with game and good bows and arrows. But very soon each wanted more than his share; and Indians quarrelled with Indians, and some were killed, and others were wounded. Then the Great Spirit made a very good word, and put it in every Indians breast, to tell us when we have done good, or when we have done bad; and that word has never told a lie.

"Friends! whenever you have stole, or got drunk, or lied, that good word has told you that you were bad Indians, and made you afraid of good Indians; and made you ashamed and look down.

"Friends! your crime is greater than all those:—you have killed an Indian in a time of peace; and made the wind hear his groans, and the earth drink his blood. You are bad Indians! Yes, you are very bad Indians; and what can you do? If you go into the woods to live alone, the ghost of John Jemison will follow you, crying, blood! blood! and will give you no peace! If you go to the land of your nation, there that ghost will attend you, and say to your relatives, see my murderers! If you plant, it will blast your corn; if you hunt, it will scare your game; and when you are asleep, its groans, and the sight of an avenging tomahawk, will awaken you! What can you do? Deserving of death, you cannot live here; and to fly from your country, to leave all your relatives, and to abandon all that you have known to be pleasant and dear, must be keener than an arrow, more bitter than gall, more terrible than death! And how must we feel?—Your path will be muddy; the woods will be dark; the lightnings will glance down the trees by your side, and you will start at every sound! peace has left you, and you must be wretched.

"Friends, hear me, and take my advice. Return with us to your homes. Offer to the Great Spirit your best wampum, and try to be good Indians! And, if those whom you have bereaved shall claim your lives as their only satisfaction, surrender them cheerfully, and die like good Indians. And—" Here Jack, highly incensed, interrupted the old man, and bade him stop speaking or he would take his life. Affrighted at the appearance of so much desperation, the company hastened towards home, and left Doctor and Jack to consult their own feelings.

As soon as they were alone, Jack said to Doctor, "I had rather die here, than leave my country and friends! Put the muzzle of your rifle into my mouth, and I will put the muzzle of mine into yours, and at a given signal we will discharge them, and rid ourselves at once of all the troubles under which we now labor, and satisfy the claims which justice holds against us."

Doctor heard the proposition, and after a moment's pause, made the following reply:—"I am as sensible as you can be of the unhappy situation in which we have placed ourselves. We are bad Indians. We have forfeited our lives, and must expect in some way to atone for our crime: but, because we are bad and miserable, shall we make ourselves worse? If we were now innocent, and in a calm reflecting moment should kill ourselves, that act would make us bad, and deprive us of our share of the good hunting in the land where our fathers have gone! What would Little Beard* say to us on our arrival at his cabin? He would say, 'Bad Indians! Cowards! You were afraid to wait till we wanted your help! Go (Jogo) to where snakes will lie in your path; where the panthers will starve

* Little Beard was a Chief who died in 1806.

you, by devouring the venison; and where you will be naked and suffer with the cold! Jogo, (go,) none but the brave and good Indians live here!' I cannot think of performing an act that will add to my wretchedness. It is hard enough for me to suffer here, and have good hunting hereafter—worse to lose the whole."

Upon this, Jack withdrew his proposal. They went on about two miles, and then turned about and came home. Guilty and uneasy, they lurked about Squawky Hill near a fortnight, and then went to Cattaraugus, and were gone six weeks. When they came back, Jack's wife earnestly requested him to remove his family to Tonnewonta; but he remonstrated against her project, and utterly declined going. His wife and family, however, tired of the tumult by which they were surrounded, packed up their effects in spite of what he could say, and went off.

Jack deliberated a short time upon the proper course for himself to pursue, and finally, rather than leave his old home, he ate a large quantity of muskrat root, and died in 10 or 12 hours. His family being immediately notified of his death, returned to attend the burial, and is yet living at Squawky Hill.

Nothing was ever done with Doctor, who continued to live quietly at Squawky Hill till sometime in the year 1819, when he died of Consumption.

15

Micah Brooks, Esq. volunteers to get the Title to her Land confirmed to herself.—She is Naturalized.—Great Council of Chiefs, &c. in September 1823.—She Disposes of her Reservation.—Reserves a Tract 2 miles long, and 1 mile wide, &c.—The Consideration how Paid, &c.

IN 1816, Micah Brooks, Esq. of Bloomfield, Ontario county, was recommended to me (as it was said) by a Mr. Ingles, to be a man of candor, honesty and integrity, who would by no means cheat me out of a cent. Mr. Brooks soon after, came to my house and informed me that he was disposed to assist me in regard to my land, by procuring a legislative act that would invest me with full power to dispose of it for my own benefit, and give as sample a title as could be given by any citizen of the state. He observed that as it was then situated, it was of but little value, because it was not in my power to dispose of it, let my necessities be ever so great. He then proposed to take the agency of the business upon himself, and to get the title of one half of my reservation vested in me personally, upon the condition that, as a reward for his services, I would give him the other half.

I sent for my son John, who on being consulted, objected to my going into any bargain with Mr. Brooks, without the advice and consent of Mr. Thomas Clute, who then lived on my land and near me. Mr. Clute was accordingly called on, to whom Mr. Brooks repeated his former statement, and added, that he would get an act passed in the Congress of the

153

United States, that would invest me with all the rights and immunities of a citizen, so far as it respected my property. Mr. Clute, suspecting that some plan was in operation that would deprive me of my possessions, advised me to have nothing to say on the subject to Mr. Brooks, till I had seen Esquire Clute, of Squawky Hill. Soon after this Thomas Clute saw Esq. Clute, who informed him that the petition for my naturalization would be presented to the Legislature of this State, instead of being sent to Congress; and that the object would succeed to his and my satisfaction. Mr. Clute then observed to his brother, Esq. Clute, that as the sale of Indian lands, which had been reserved, belonged exclusively to the United States, an act of the Legislature of New-York could have no effect in securing to me a title to my reservation, or in depriving me of my property. They finally agreed that I should sign a petition to Congress, praying for my naturalization, and for the confirmation of the title of my land to me, my heirs, & c.

Mr. Brooks came with the petition: I signed it, and it was witnessed by Thomas Clute, and two others, and then returned to Mr. Brooks, who presented it to the Legislature of this state at its session in the winter of 1816–17. On the 19th of April, 1817, an act was passed for my naturalization, and ratifying and confirming the title of my land, agreeable to the tenor of the petition, which act Mr. Brooks presented to me on the first day of May following.

Thomas Clute having examined the law, told me that it would probably answer, though it was not according to the agreement made by Mr. Brooks, and Esq. Clute and himself, for me. I then executed to Micah Brooks and Jellis Clute, a deed of all my land lying east of the picket line on the Gardow reservation, containing about 7000 acres.

It is proper in this place to observe, in relation to Mr. Thomas Clute, that my son John, a few months before his death, advised me to take him for my guardian, (as I had become old and incapable of managing my property,) and to compensate him for his trouble by giving him a lot of land on the west side of my reservation where he should choose it. I accordingly took my son's advice, and Mr. Clute has ever since been faithful and honest in all his advice and dealings with, and for, myself and family.

In the month of August, 1817, Mr. Brooks and Esq. Clute again came to me with a request that I would give them a lease of the land which I had already deeded to them, together with the other part of my reservation, excepting and reserving to myself only about 4000 acres.

At this time I informed Thomas Clute of what John had advised, and recommended me to do, and that I had consulted my daughters on the subject, who had approved of the measure. He readily agreed to assist me; whereupon I told him he was entitled to a lot of land, and might select as John had mentioned. He accordingly at that time took such a piece as he chose, and the same has ever since been reserved for him in all the land contracts which I have made.

On the 24th of August, 1817, I leased to Micah Brooks and Jellis Clute, the whole of my original reservation, except 4000 acres, and Thomas Clute's lot. Finding their title still incomplete, on account of the United States government and Seneca Chiefs not having sanctioned my acts, they solicited me to renew the contract, and have the conveyance made to them in such a manner as that they should thereby be constituted sole proprietors of the soil.

In the winter of 1822–3, I agreed with them, that if they would get the chiefs of our nation, and a United States Commissioner of Indian Lands, to meet in council at Moscow, Livingston county, N. Y. and there concur in my agreement, that I would sell to them all my right and title to the Gardow reservation, with the exception of a tract for my own benefit, two miles long, and one mile wide, lying on the river where I should choose it; and also reserving Thomas Clute's lot. This arrangement was agreed upon, and the council assembled at the place appointed, on the 3d or 4th day of September, 1823.

That council consisted of Major Carrol, who had been appointed by the President to dispose of my lands, Judge Howell and N. Gorham, of Canandaigua, (who acted in concert with Maj. Carrol,) Jasper Parrish, Indian Agent, Horatio Jones, Interpreter, and a great number of Chiefs.

The bargain was assented to unanimously, and a deed given to H. B. Gibson, Micah Brooks and Jellis Clute, of the whole Gardow tract, excepting the last mentioned reservations, which was signed by myself and upwards of twenty Chiefs.

The land which I now own, is bounded as follows:— Beginning at the center of the Great Slide* and running west one mile, thence north two miles, thence east about one mile to Genesee river, thence south on the west bank of Genesee river to the place of beginning.

In consideration of the above sale, the purchasers have bound themselves, their heirs, assigns, &c. to pay to me, my heirs or successors, three hundred dollars a year forever.

Whenever the land which I have reserved, shall be sold, the income of it is to be equally divided amongst the members of the Seneca nation, without any reference to tribes or families.

* The Great Slide of the bank of Genesee river is a curiosity worthy of the attention of the traveller. In the month of May, 1817, a portion of land thickly covered with timber, situated at the upper end of the Gardow flats, on the west side of the river, all of a sudden gave way, and with a tremendous crash, slid into the bed of the river, which it so completely filled, that the stream formed a new passage on the east side of it, where it continues to run, without overflowing the slide. This slide, as it now lies, contains 22 acres, and has a considerable share of the timber that formerly covered it, still standing erect upon it, and growing.

16

Conclusion.—Review of her Life.—Reflections on the loss of Liberty.—Care she took to preserve her Health.—Indians' abstemiousness in Drinking, after the French War.—Care of their Lives, &c.—General use of Spirits.—Her natural Strength.—Purchase of her first Cow.—Means by which she has been supplied with Food.—Suspicions of her having been a Witch.—Her Constancy.—Number of Children.—Number Living.—Their Residence.—Closing Reflection.

WHEN I review my life, the privations that I have suffered, the hardships I have endured, the vicissitudes I have passed, and the complete revolution that I have experienced in my manner of living; when I consider my reduction from a civilized to a savage state, and the various steps by which that process has been effected, and that my life has been prolonged, and my health and reason spared, it seems a miracle that I am unable to account for, and is a tragical medley that I hope will never be repeated.

The bare loss of liberty is but a mere trifle when compared with the circumstances that necessarily attend, and are inseparably connected with it. It is the recollection of what we once were, of the friends, the home, and the pleasures that we have left or lost; the anticipation of misery, the appearance of wretchedness, the anxiety for freedom, the hope of release, the devising of means of escaping, and the vigilance with which we watch our keepers, that constitute the nauseous dregs of the bitter cup of slavery. I am sensible, however, that no one can pass from a state of freedom to that of slavery, and in the last situation rest perfectly contented; but as every one knows that great exertions of the mind tend directly to debilitate the body, it will appear obvious that we ought, when confined, to exert all our faculties to promote our present comfort, and let future days provide their own sacrifices. In regard to ourselves, just as we feel, we are.

For the preservation of my life to the present time I am indebted to an excellent constitution, with which I have been blessed in as great a degree as any other person. After I arrived to years of understanding, the care of my own health was one of my principal studies; and by avoiding exposures to wet and cold, by temperance in eating, abstaining from the use of spirits, and shunning the excesses to which I was frequently exposed, I effected my object beyond what I expected. I have never once been sick till within a year or two, only as I have related.

Spirits and tobacco I have never used, and I have never once attended an Indian frolic. When I was taken prisoner, and for sometime after that, spirits was not known; and when it was first introduced, it was in small quantities, and used only by the Indians; so that it was a long time before the Indian women begun to even taste it.

After the French war, for a number of years, it was the practice of the Indians of our tribe to send to Niagara and get two or three kegs of rum, (in all six or eight gallons,) and hold a frolic as long as it lasted. When the rum was brought to the town, all the Indians collected, and before a drop was drank, gave all their knives, tomahawks, guns, and other instruments of war, to one Indian, whose business it was to bury them in a private place, keep them concealed, and remain perfectly sober till the frolic was ended. Having thus divested themselves, they commenced drinking, and continued their frolic till every drop was consumed. If any of them became quarrelsome, or got to fighting, those who were sober enough bound them upon the ground, where they were obliged to lie till they got sober, and then were unbound. When the fumes of the spirits had left the company, the sober Indian returned to each the instruments with which they had entrusted him, and all went home satisfied. A frolic of that kind was held but once a year, and that at the time the Indians quit their hunting, and come in with their deer-skins.

In those frolics the women never participated. Soon after the revolutionary war, however, spirits became common in our tribe, and has been used indiscriminately by both sexes; though there are not so frequent instances of intoxication amongst the squaws as amongst the Indians.

To the introduction and use of that baneful article, which has made such devastation in our tribes, and threatens the extinction of our people, (the Indians,) I can with the greatest propriety impute the whole of my misfortune in losing my three sons. But as I have before observed, not even the love of life will restrain an Indian from sipping the poison that he knows will destroy him. The voice of nature, the rebukes of reason, the advice of parents, the expostulations of friends, and the numerous instances of sudden death, are all insufficient to reclaim an Indian, who has once experienced the exhilarating and inebriating effects of spirits, from seeking his grave in the bottom of his bottle!

My strength has been great for a woman of my size, otherwise I must long ago have died under the burdens which I was obliged to carry. I learned to carry loads on my back, in a strap placed across my forehead, soon after my captivity; and continue to carry in the same way. Upwards of thirty years ago, with the help of my young children, I backed all the boards that were used about my house from Allen's mill at the outlet of Silver Lake, a distance of five miles. I have planted, hoed, and harvested corn every season but one since I was taken prisoner. Even this present fall (1823) I have husked my corn and backed it into the house.

The first cow that I ever owned, I bought of a squaw sometime after the revolution. It had been stolen from the enemy. I had owned it but a few days when it fell into a hole, and almost died before we could get it out. After this, the squaw wanted to be recanted, but as I would not give up the cow, I gave her money enough to make, when added to the sum which I paid her at first, thirty-five dollars. Cows were plenty on the Ohio, when I lived there, and of good quality.

For provisions I have never suffered since I came upon

the flats; nor have I ever been in debt to any other hands than my own for the plenty that I have shared.

My vices, that have been suspected, have been but few. It was believed for a long time, by some of our people, that I was a great witch; but they were unable to prove my guilt, and consequently I escaped the certain doom of those who are convicted of that crime, which, by Indians, is considered as heinous as murder. Some of my children had light brown hair, and tolerable fair skin, which used to make some say that I stole them; yet as I was ever conscious of my own constancy, I never thought that any one really believed that I was guilty of adultery.

I have been the mother of eight children; three of whom are now living, and I have at this time thirty-nine grand children, and fourteen great-grand children, all living in the neighborhood of Genesee River, and at Buffalo.

I live in my own house, and on my own land, with my youngest daughter, Polly, who is married to George Chongo, and has three children.

My daughter Nancy, who is married to Billy Green, lives about 80 rods south of my house, and has seven children.

My other daughter, Betsey, is married to John Green, has seven children, and resides 80 rods north of my house.

Thus situated in the midst of my children, I expect I shall soon leave the world, and make room for the rising generation. I feel the weight of years with which I am loaded, and am sensible of my daily failure in seeing, hearing and strength; but my only anxiety is for my family. If my family will live happily, and I can be exempted from trouble while I have to stay, I feel as though I could lay down in peace a life that has been checked in almost every hour, with troubles of deeper dye, than are commonly experienced by mortals.

BIBLIOGRAPHY

Manuscripts, Special Collections, Historical Society and
Museum Collections, Exhibitions, and Demonstrations

BUFFALO AND ERIE HISTORICAL SOCIETY, Buffalo, N.Y.
Parker, Arthur C. Manuscript Collections. Material credited to
Laura M. Wright's papers (typed, unsigned copy).
Sutherland, Margaret Brandt. *The Life of Mary Jemison: Narrative
Poem.* Presented in pageantry by the Castile Historical Society
annually at Letchworth State Park Castile, N.Y. First drama-
tized in 1953. Castile, N.Y.: "The Castilian" Press, 1955.
Whalen, Will W. *The Red Light of Buchanan Valley.* Orrtanna,
Adams County, Pa.: White Squaw Publishing Company, 1923.

WILLIAM PRIOR LETCHWORTH MUSEUM, Castile, N.Y.
Newspaper articles.
Cook, Tom. "White Woman of Genesee Legend Endures." *Out-
doors,* 1984, 2–4.
Jamieson, Monica V. "Kin of Mary Jamieson Hold Onondaga Re-
union." *Brantford Expositor,* June, 1956.

MILNE LIBRARY, State University College of Arts and Sciences at
Geneseo, N.Y.
William Prior Letchworth Collection. The collection belongs to the
Letchworth State Park and William Prior Letchworth Museum,
but is housed at the State University of New York at Geneseo.

NATIONAL MUSEUM OF AMERICAN HISTORY, Smithsonian Institution,
Washington, D.C.
Exhibition. "After the Revolution. Getting Dressed: Fashionable
Appearance, 1750–1800." 1987.

NATIONAL MUSEUM OF NATURAL HISTORY, Smithsonian Institution, Washington, D.C.
Anthropological Archives, Iroquois files.
Anthropology Collection, Iroquois materials.
Bureau of Ethnology Collections.

NATIONAL SOCIETY DAUGHTERS OF THE AMERICAN REVOLUTION, Washington, D.C.
Seaver family. "Family Skeletons and Ghosts." "Hunt" and "Everett" families, copied by David Seaver from genealogies printed at Boston, Mass. (Manuscript collection.)
Seaver, Jesse. "The Seaver Genealogy: A Genealogy, History, and Directory." Philadelphia, 1924. (Typescript.)
Trask, William Blake. *A Genealogy of Robert Seaver: The Seaver Family: A Genealogy of Robert Seaver of Roxbury of Massachusetts and Some of his Descendants.* Boston: David Clapp and Son, 1872.

NEW YORK PUBLIC LIBRARY, Special Collections, New York, N.Y.
"Map of Ho-De-No-Saw-Nee-Ga or the People of the Long House, compiled about 1851 by Lewis H. Morgan and Ely S. Parker, A Seneca Sachem, from several French Maps of 1720 or Earlier."

PEABODY MUSEUM, Harvard University, Cambridge, Mass.
Iroquois Collections.
Northeast Indian Collections.

ROCHESTER MUSEUM AND SCIENCE CENTER, Rochester, N.Y.
Rose, Richard. Unpublished paper, "The Lewis Henry Morgan collection at the Rochester Museum."
Exhibits on Iroquois and Native American Life.

RUSH RHEES LIBRARY, University of Rochester, Rochester, N.Y.
Rare Books and Special Collections.
Bartlett, Charles E. "Unto My People. Mary Jemison White Woman of the Genesee: An Outdoor Drama Based on the Life of Mary Jemison. Program for play July 29–31, ca. 1950s.
Morgan, Lewis Henry. Papers (1839–1885).

PRIMARY SOURCES AND MATERIALS PRINTED BEFORE 1900

Abler, Thomas S. ed. *Chainbreaker: The Revolutionary War Memoirs of Governor Blacksnake as told to Benjamin Williams.* Lincoln: University of Nebraska Press, 1989.
Anderson, Arthur J. O., and Charles E. Dibble, trans. and eds. *The War of Conquest: How It Was Waged Here in Mexico, The*

Aztecs' Own Story as Given to Fr. Bernardio de Sahagún, Salt Lake City: University of Utah Press, 1978.

Arber, Edward, and A. G. Bradley, eds. *Travels and Works of Captain John Smith: President of Virginia, and Admiral of New England, 1580–1631.* 2 vols. Edinburgh: John Grant, 1910.

Axtell, James, ed. *The Native American People of the East.* West Haven, Conn.: Pendulum Press, 1973.

————. *The Indian Peoples of Eastern America: A Documentary History of the Sexes.* New York: Oxford University Press, 1981.

Baker, C. Alice. *True Stories of New England Captives Carried to Canada during the Old French and Indian Wars.* Cambridge: n.p., 1897.

Barbour, Philip L., ed. *The Complete Works of Captain John Smith (1580–1631) in Three Volumes.* Chapel Hill: University of North Carolina Press, 1986.

Beers, F. W., ed. *Gazetteer and Biographical Record of Genesee County, N.Y., 1788–1890.* Syracuse: J. W. Vose and Co., 1890.

Bruchac, Joseph, ed. *Songs from This Earth on Turtle's Back: Contemporary American Indian Poetry.* Greenfield Center, N.Y.: Greenfield Review Press, 1983.

Chafe, Wallace L. *Handbook of the Seneca Language.* Service Bulletin 388. Albany: New York State Museum and Science, 1963.

Child, Lydia Maria. *Hobomok and Other Writings on Indians.* Edited by Carolyn L. Karcher. New Brunswick, N.J.: Rutgers University Press, 1986.

Colden, Cadwallader. *The History of the Five Indian Nations Depending on the Province of New-York in America.* 1727 and 1747. Reprint. Ithaca, N. Y.: Cornell University Press, 1986.

Commager, Henry Steele, and Richard B. Morris, eds. *The Spirit of 'Seventy-Six: The Story of the American Revolution as Told by Participants.* New York: Harper and Row, 1967.

Converse, Harriet Maxwell. *Myths and Legends of the New York State Iroquois.* Museum Bulletin 125. Education Department Bulletin 437. 1908. Reprint. Albany: University of the State of New York, 1974.

Cooper, James Fenimore. *The Last of the Mohicans: A Narrative of 1757.* 1826. 1919 edition illustrated N. C. Wyeth. Reprint. New York: Charles Scribner's Sons, 1986.

Cornplanter, Jesse J., of the Senecas. *Legends of the Longhouse.* Told to Sah-Nee-Weh, the White Sister [Mrs. Walter A. Hendricks]. Philadelphia: J. B. Lippincott, 1938.

Description of the Settlement of the Genesee Country, in the State of New-York. In a Series of Letters from a Gentleman to His Friend. New York: T. and J. Swords, 1799.

Doddridge, Joseph. *Notes on the Settlement and Indian Wars of the*

Western Parts of Virginia and Pennsylvania from 1763–1783. Pittsburgh: John S. Ritenour and William T. Lindsay, 1912.

Doty, Lockwood L. *A History of Livingston County, New York: From Its Earliest Traditions, to Its Part in the War for Our Union*. Geneseo: Edward E. Doty, 1876.

Drake, Samuel G. *Tragedies of the Wilderness; or the True and Authentic Narratives of Captives, Who Have Been Carried Away by the Indians from the Various Frontier Settlements of the United States, from the Earliest to the Present Time*. Boston: Antiquarian Bookstore and Institute, 1846.

————. *Biography and History of the Indians of North America, from Its First Discovery*. Boston: Benjamin B. Muzzey, 1851.

————. *Indian Captivities: Life in the Wigwam; Being True Narratives of Captives Who Have Been Carried Away by the Indians, from the Frontier Settlements of the United States, from the Earliest Period to the Present Time*. New York: Miller, Orton and Co. 1857.

Drimmer, Frederick. *Captured by the Indians: Fifteen Firsthand Accounts, 1750–1870*. 1961. Reprint. New York: Dover Publications, 1985.

Drinnon, Richard, ed. *Memoirs of a Captivity among the Indians of North America: John Dunn Hunter*. 1824. Reprint. New York: Schocken, 1973.

Ellet, Mrs. E[lizabeth] F. *Pioneer Women of the West*. New York, 1852.

Evans, Charles, comp. *American Bibliography: A Chronological Dictionary of All Books, Pamphlets, and Periodical Publications Printed in the United States of America From the Genesis of Printing in 1639 Down to and Including the Years 1820*. 14 vols. New York: P. Smith, 1941–59.

Fenton, William N., ed. "Documents: Seneca Indians by Asher Wright (1859)." From American Board of Commissioners for Foreign Missions. *Ethnohistory* 4 (Summer, 1957): 302–20.

————. *Parker on the Iroquois: Iroquois Uses of Maize and Other Food Plants; The Code of Handsome Lake, the Seneca Prophet; The Constitution of the Five Nations*. Reprint. Syracuse: Syracuse University Press, 1968.

Fogelson, Raymond D., et al., eds. *Contributions to Anthropology: Selected Papers of A. Irving Hallowell*. Chicago: University of Chicago Press, 1976.

Froncek, Thomas, ed. *Voices from the Wilderness: The Frontiersman's Own Story*. New York: McGraw-Hill, 1974.

Frost, John. *Thrilling Adventures among the Indians*. Philadelphia: J. W. Bradley, 1851.

————— . *Daring and Heroic Deeds of American Women*. Philadelphia: G. G. Evans, 1860.

————— . *Pioneer Mothers of the West or Daring and Heroic Deeds of American Women*. Boston: Lee and Shepard, 1869.

Gardner, Jeanne Le Monnier. *Mary Jemison: Seneca Captive*. Illustrated by Robert Parker. New York: Harcourt, Brace and World, 1966.

Hardenbergh, John L. *The Journal of Lieut. John L. Hardenbergh of the Second New York Continental Regiment from May 1 to October 3, 1779, in General Sullivan's Campaign Against the Western Indians*. Auburn, N.Y.: n.p., 1879.

Harris, George H. *Aboriginal Occupation of the Lower Genesee Country*. Rochester, N.Y.: n.p., 1884.

Heckewelder, John. *History, Manners, and Customs of the Indian Nations Who Once Inhabited Pennsylvania and the Neighboring States*. Edited by Dale Van Every. 1819. Reprint. New York: Arno Press and The New York Times, 1971.

Hewitt, J. N. B., ed. *Iroquoian Cosmology*, pt. 1. *Twenty-first Annual Report of the Bureau of American Ethnology*, 1899–1900. Washington: Government Printing Office, 1903.

————— . "Seneca Fiction, Legends, and Myths, Part I." *Thirty-second Annual Report of the U.S. Bureau of Ethnology, 1910–1911. Washington: Government Printing Office, 1918*.

Hunter, John D. *Manners and Customs of Several Indian Tribes Located West of the Mississippi*. 1823. Reprint. Minneapolis: Ross and Haines, 1957.

James, Edwin. *A Narrative of the Captivity and Adventures of John Tanner, (U.S. Interpreter at the Saut De Ste. Marie,) During Thirty Years Residence among the Indians in the Interior of North America*. Introduction by Noel Loomis. 1830. Reprint. Minneapolis: Ross and Haines, 1956.

Jennings, Francis, William N. Fenton, et al., eds. *The History and Culture of Iroquois Diplomacy: An Interdisciplinary Guide to the Treaties of the Six Nations and Their League*. Syracuse, N.Y.: Syracuse University Press, 1985.

Journals of the Military Expedition of Major General John D. Sullivan Against the Six Nations of Indians in 1779 with Records of Centennial Celebrations. Auburn, N.Y.: Knapp, Peck and Thompson, 1887.

Katz, Jane B., ed. *I Am the Fire of Time: The Voices of Native American Women*. New York: E. P. Dutton, 1977.

Ketchum, William. *An Authentic and Comprehensive History of Buffalo with Some Accounts of Its Early Inhabitants Both Savage and Civilized*. 2 vols. Buffalo, N.Y.: Rockwell, Baker and Hill, 1864.

Kupperman, Karen Ordahl, ed. *Captain John Smith: A Select Edition of His Writings.* Chapel Hill: University of North Carolina Press, 1988.

Lafitau, Joseph François. *Customs of the American Indians Compared with the Customs of Primitive Tribes.* Edited and translated by William N. Fenton and Elizabeth L. Moore. 2 vols. 1724. Toronto: Champlain Society, 1974–1977.

Lenski, Lois. *Indian Captive: The Story of Mary Jemison.* 15th printing. Philadelphia: J. B. Lippincott, 1941.

———. *Der Abenteuer der jungen "Maisblute": ein jungen Mädchen wird Indianerin.* Translated into German by Josef Karl Thiel. Darmstadt: F. Schneekluth, 195? and ca. 1960.

———. *Indian Captive: The Story of Mary Jemison.* New York: Fredrick A. Stokes, 1941.

Levernier, James, and Hennig Cohen, eds. *The Indians and Their Captives.* Westport, Conn.: Greenwood Press, 1977.

Lincoln, Charles, ed. *Narratives of the Indian Wars, 1675–1699.* New York: Charles Scribner's Sons, 1913.

Lossing, Benson J. *The Pictorial Field-Book of the Revolution; or Illustrations, by Pen and Pencil, of the History, Biography, Scenery, Relics, and the Traditions of the War of Independence.* 2 vols. New York: Harper and Brothers, 1869.

———. *The Empire State: A Compendious History of the Commonwealth of New York.* Hartford, Conn.: American Publishing Co., 1892.

Marshall, Orsamus H. "The Niagra Frontier." *Publications of the Buffalo Historical Society* 2 (1880): 395–425.

Meginness, John F. *Biography of Frances Slocum: The Lost Sister of Wyoming.* Williamsport, Pa.: Heller Bros. Printing House. 1891.

Mithun, Marianne, and Hanni Woodbury, eds. *Northern Iroquoian Texts.* International Journal of Linguistics, Native American Texts Series, IJAL-NATS monograph no. 4. Chicago: University of Chicago Press, 1980.

Morgan, Lewis H. *League of the Ho-dé-no-sau-nee or Iroquois.* Edited by Herbert M. Lloyd. 2 vols. in one. New York: Dodd, Mead and Co., 1904.

Murdock, George P. *Outline of World Cultures.* 6th ed., rev. New Haven, Conn.: Human Relations Area Files, 1983.

Murdock, George P., et al. *Outline of Cultural Materials.* 5th ed., rev. New Haven, Conn. Human Relations Area Files, 1982.

"Museum Notes." *Buffalo Historical Society* 2, no. 2 (April–September, 1933).

Nabokov, Peter, ed. *Native American Testimony: An Anthology of*

Indian and White Relations, First Encounter of Dispossession.
New York: Thomas Y. Crowell, 1978.

Parker, Arthur C. "The Code of Handsome Lake, the Seneca
Prophet." *Education Department Bulletin* (Albany, N.Y., Museum) 163, no. 350 (November 1, 1912).

———. *Seneca Myths and Folk Tales.* Buffalo, N.Y.: Buffalo Historical Society, 1923.

———. *The History of the Seneca Indians.* Empire State Historical
Publication 43. 1926. Reprint. Port Washington, N.Y.: Ira J.
Friedman, 1967.

Peckham, Howard Henry. *Captured by Indians: True Tales of Pioneer Survivors.* New Brunswick, N.J.: Rutgers University
Press, 1954.

Pierce, M. B. ("A Chief of the Seneca Nation, and a Member of
Dartmouth College"). "Address on the Present Condition and
Prospects of the Aboriginal Inhabitants of North America, with
Particular Reference to the Seneca Nation." N.p.: Steele's
Press, 1838.

Reid, Arthur. *Reminiscences of the Revolution, or Le Loup's Bloody
Trail from Salem to Fort Edward.* Utica, N.Y.: Roberts, Book
and Job Printer, 1859.

Rothenberg, Jerome, ed. *Shaking the Pumpkin: Traditional Poetry
of Indian North Americans.* New York: Doubleday, 1972.

Seaver, James Everett. *A Narrative of the Life of Mrs. Mary Jemison,
Who was taken by the Indians, in the year 1755, when only about
twelve years of age, and has continued to reside amongst them to the
present time.* Canandaigua, N.Y.: J. D. Bemis and Co., 1824.

———. *Deh-he-wä-mis: or A Narrative of the Life of Mary Jemison:
Otherwise Called the White Woman, Who Was Taken Captive by
the Indians in MDCCLV; and Who Continued with Them Seventy-
Eight Years, Containing an Account of the Murder of Her Father
and His Family, Her Marriages and Sufferings, Indian Barbarities, Customs and Traditions. Carefully Taken from Her Own
Words by James E. Seaver.* 2d ed. Batavia, N.Y.: William Seaver
and Son, 1842.

———. *Life of Mary Jemison: Deh-he-wä-mis.* 4th ed. with Geographical and Explanatory Notes. New York and Auburn:
Miller, Orton and Mulligan; Rochester: D. M. Dewey, 1856.

———. *Life of Mary Jemison: Deh-he-wä-mis.* Buffalo: William P.
Letchworth, 1880.

———. *A Narrative of the Life of Mary Jemison: The White Woman
of the Genesee.* 21st ed., revised by Charles Delamater Vail.
New York: American Scenic and Historic Preservation Society,
1918.

—————. *A Narrative of the Life of Mary Jemison: The White Woman of the Genesee.* 22d ed., revised by Charles Delamater Vail. New York: American Scenic and Historic Preservation Society, 1925.

—————. *A Narrative of the Life of Mrs. Mary Jemison.* Introduction by Allen W. Trelease. Gloucester, Mass.: Peter Smith, 1975.

—————. *A Narrative of the Life of Mrs. Mary Jemison, Who Was Taken by the Indians, in the Year 1755, When Only about Twelve Years of Age, and Has Continued to Reside amongst Them to the Present Time.* 1824 and 1856. Narratives of North American Indian Captivity, no. 41. New York: Garland Publishing, 1977.

Slotkin, Richard, and James K. Folsom, eds. *So Dreadfull a Judgment: Puritan Responses to King Philip's War, 1676–1677.* Middletown, Conn.: Wesleyan University Press, 1978.

Smith, Erminnie A. *Myths of the Iroquois.* Washington, D.C.: Government Printing Office, 1883.

Smith, William. *Expedition Against the Ohio Indians, An Historical Account of the Expedition Against the Ohio Indians, in the Year 1764, Under the Command of Henry Bouquet, Esq.* 1765. Reprint. Ann Arbor, Mich.: University Microfilms, 1966.

Stern, Bernard J. "The Letters of Asher Wright to Lewis Henry Morgan." *American Anthropologist* 35 (January–March, 1933): 138–45.

Sullivan's Campaign 1779. Journals, Notes and Biography. Cayuga County Historical Collections 1 (1879).

Tanner, Helen Hornbeck, ed. *Atlas of Great Lakes Indian History.* Norman: University of Oklahoma Press, 1987.

Thwaites, Reuben Gold, ed. *The Jesuit Relations and Allied Documents: Travel and Explorations of the Jesuit Missionaries in New France, 1610–1791; the Original French, Latin, and Italian Texts, with English Translations and Notes.* 73 vols. Cleveland: Burrows Brothers, 1896–1901. Reprint. Pageant, N.Y., 1959.

Tooker, Elisabeth. *The Indians of the Northeast: A Critical Bibliography.* Bloomington: Indiana University Press, 1978.

—————. ed. *An Iroquois Source Book.* 3 vols. New York: Garland Publishers, 1985–86.

A True History of the Captivity and Restoration of Mrs. Mary Rowlandson, a Minister's Wife in New England. 1682. Reprint. New York: Garland Publishing, 1977.

Turner, Fredrick W., III, ed. *The Portable North American Indian Reader.* Rev. ed. New York: Penguin Books, 1981.

Vail, R. W. G. *The Voice of the Old Frontier.* New York: Yoseloff, 1949.

—————. ed. "The Western Campaign of 1779: The Diary of Quartermaster Sergeant Moses Sproule of the Third New Jersey

Regiment in the Sullivan Expedition of the Revolutionary War, May 17—October 17, 1779." *New York Historical Society Quarterly* 41 (January, 1957): 35–69.

VanDerBeets, Richard, ed. *Held Captive by Indians: Selective Narratives, 1642–1836.* Knoxville, Tenn.: University of Tennessee Press, 1973.

Vaughan, Alden T. *Narratives of North American Indian Captivity: A Selective Bibliography.* New York: Garland Publishing, 1983.

Vaughan, Alden T., and Edward W. Clark, eds. *Puritans among the Indians: Accounts of Captivity and Redemption, 1676–1724.* Cambridge, Mass.: Harvard University Press, 1981.

Wallace, Anthony F. C., ed. "Halliday Jackson's Journal to the Seneca Indians, 1798–1800." Reprint. *Pennsylvania History* 19 (April, 1952, and July, 1952).

Wallace, Paul A. W. *The White Roots of Peace.* 1946. Reprint. Saranac Lake, N.Y.: Chauncy Press, 1986.

Washburn, Wilcomb E., ed. *The Indian and the White Man.* Garden City, N.Y.: Anchor Books, 1964.

———. *The Garland Library of Narratives of North American Indian Captivities.* 111 vols. New York: Garland Publishing, 1976–1983.

Wright, Albert Hazen, ed. *The Sullivan Expedition of 1779: Contemporary Newspaper Comment and Letters, Pt. I, Preliminary Correspondence and Raids.* Studies in History, no. 5. Ithaca, N. Y.: A. H. Wright, 1943.

SECONDARY WORKS

Acherknecht, Erwin H. "'White Indians': Psychological Peculiarities of White Children Abducted and Reared by North American Indians." *Bulletin of the History of Medicine* 15 (January, 1944): 15–36.

Albers, Patricia, and Beatrice Medicine. *The Hidden Half: Studies of Plains Indian Women.* Washington; D.C.: University Press of America, 1983.

Alden, John Richard. *The American Revolution, 1775–1783.* New York: Harper and Brothers, 1954.

Antler, Joyce. *Lucy Sprague Mitchell: The Making of a Modern Woman.* New Haven: Yale University Press, 1987.

Armitage, Susan, and Elizabeth Jameson, eds. *The Women's West.* Norman: University of Oklahoma, 1987.

Axtell, James. "Through a Glass Darkly: Colonial Attitudes Toward the Native Americans." *American Indian Culture and Research Journal* 1, no. 1 (1974): 17–28.

———. *After Columbus: Essays in the Ethnohistory of Colonial North America.* New York: Oxford University Press, 1988.

————. "The Ethnohistory of Early America: A Review Essay," *William and Mary Quarterly*, 3d ser., 35 (1978): 110–44.

————. *The European and the Indian: Essays in the Ethnohistory of Colonial North America*. New York: Oxford University Press, 1981.

————. *The Invasion Within: The Conquest of Cultures in Colonial America*. New York: Oxford University Press, 1985.

Bailyn, Bernard. *The Peopling of British North America: An Introduction*. New York: Knopf, 1986.

Bailyn, Bernard, with Barbara De Wolfe. *Voyagers to the West: A Passage in the Peopling of America on the Eve of the Revolution*. New York: Knopf, 1986.

Barnett, Louise. *The Ignoble Savage: American Literary Racism, 1790–1890*. Westport, Conn.: Greenwood Press, 1975.

Bataille, Gretchen M., and Kathleen Mullen Sands. *American Indian Women: Telling Their Lives*. Lincoln: University of Nebraska Press, 1984.

Baym, Nina. *Woman's Fiction: A Guide to Novels by and about Women in America, 1820–1870*. Ithaca, N. Y.: University of Cornell Press, 1978.

————. *Novels, Readers, and Reviewers: Responses to Fiction in Antebellum America*. Ithaca, N.Y.: Cornell University Press, 1984.

Beauchamp, William M. "Iroquois Women." *Journal of American Folk-Lore* 13 (1900): 81–91.

————. *A History of the New York Iroquois*. New York State Museum Bulletin 78. Albany: New York State Education Department, 1905.

Berkhofer, Robert F., Jr. "Faith and Factionalism among the Senecas: Theory and Ethnohistory." *Ethnohistory* 12 (Spring, 1965): 99–112.

————. *The White Man's Indian: Images of the American Indian, from Columbus to the Present*. New York: Vintage Books-Random House, 1979.

Billias, George Allan, ed. *George Washington's Generals*. New York: William Morrow, 1964.

Billington, Ray Allen. *Land of Savagery, Land of Promise: The European Image of the American Frontier in the Nineteenth Century*. New York: W. W. Norton, 1981.

Boelhower, William. *Through a Glass Darkly: Ethnic Semiosis in American Literature*. New York: Oxford University Press, 1987.

Brigham, Robert W. "Mary Jemison: 'The White Woman of the Genesee.' " "Museum Notes." *Buffalo Historical Society* 2 (April–September, 1933): 3–5.

Brose, David S., James A. Brown, and David W. Penney. *Ancient Art of the American Woodland Indians.* New York: Harry N. Abrams in association with the Detroit Institute of Art, 1985.

Brumble, H. David, III. *An Annotated Bibliography of American Indian and Eskimo Autobiographies.* Lincoln: University of Nebraska Press, 1981.

Brush, Edward Hale. *Iroquois Past and Present, I: Including Brief Sketches of Red Jacket, Cornplanter and Mary Jemison by Edward Dinwoodie Strickland.* N.p.: n.p. 1901.

Bucher, Bernadette. *Icon and Conquest: A Structural Analysis of the Illustrations of de Bry's Great Voyages.* Translated by Basia Miller Gulati. Chicago: University of Chicago Press, 1981.

Calloway, Colin G. "An Uncertain Destiny: Indian Captivities on the Upper Connecticut River." *Journal of American Studies* 17 (August, 1983): 190–210.

———. ed. *New Directions in American Indian History.* Norman: University of Oklahoma Press, 1988.

Campisi, Jack, and Laurence M. Hauptman, eds. *The Oneida Indian Experience: Two Perspectives.* Syracuse, N.Y.: Syracuse University Press, 1988.

Carleton, Phillips D. "The Indian Captivity." *American Literature* 15 (March, 1943–January, 1944): 169–80.

Chiappelli, Fredi, et al. *First Images of America: The Impact of the New World on the Old.* Vol. 1. Berkeley: University of California Press, 1976.

Clune, Henry W. *The Genesee.* New York: Holt, Rinehart and Winston, 1963.

Coleman, Emma Lewis. *New England Captives Carried to Canada: Between 1677 and 1760.* 2 vols. Portland, Me.: Southworth Press, 1925.

Cook, Tom. "The Letchworth Collection: A Survey of a 19th Century Indian Museum." In Russell A. Judkins, ed., *Iroquois Studies: A Guide to Documentary and Ethnographic Resources from Western New York and the Genesee Valley,* 1–7. Geneseo, N.Y.: Department of Anthropology, State University of New York at Geneseo, and the Geneseo Foundation, 1987.

Cott, Nancy F., and Elizabeth H. Pleck, eds. *A Heritage of Her Own: Toward a New Social History of American Women.* New York: Simon and Schuster, 1979.

Countryman, Edward. *A People in Revolution: The American Revolution and Political Society in New York, 1760–1790.* Baltimore: Johns Hopkins University, 1981.

Cronon, William. *Changes in the Land: Indians, Colonists, and the Ecology of New England.* New York: Hill and Wang, 1983.

Crosby, Alfred W., Jr. *The Columbian Exchange: Biological and Cultural Consequences of 1492.* Westport, Conn.: Greenwood Press, 1972.

Dobson, Eleanor Robinette. "Mary Jemison." In Dumas Malone, ed., *Dictionary of American Biography* 10:39–40. New York: Charles Scribner's Sons, 1933.

Dearborn, Mary V. *Pocahontas's Daughters: Gender and Ethnicity in American Culture.* New York: Oxford University Press, 1986.

D'Emilio, John, and Estelle B. Freedman. *Intimate Matters: A History of Sexuality in America.* New York: Harper and Row, 1988.

Dobyns, Henry F. *Their Number Become Thinned: Native American Population Dynamics in Eastern North America.* Knoxville: University of Tennessee Press, 1983.

Douglas, Ann. *The Feminization of American Culture.* New York: Alfred A. Knopf, 1977.

Drinnon, Richard. *White Savage: The Case of John Dunn Hunter.* New York: Schocken Books, 1972.

——— . *Facing West: The Metaphysics of Indian-Hating and Empire Building.* Minneapolis: University of Minnesota Press, 1980.

Duncan, John Donald. "Indian Slavery." In *Race Relations in British North America, 1607–1783,* edited by Bruce A. Glasrud and Alan M. Smith, 85–106. Chicago: Nelson-Hall, 1982.

Edmunds, R. David. *The Shawnee Prophet.* Lincoln: University of Nebraska Press, 1983.

Etienne, Mona, and Eleanor Leacock, eds. *Women and Colonization: Anthropological Perspectives.* New York: Praeger, 1980.

Faragher, John Mack. *Women and Men on the Overland Trail.* New Haven: Yale University Press, 1979.

Fenton, William N. *An Outline of the Seneca Ceremonies at Coldspring Longhouse.* Yale University Publications in Anthropology, no. 9 New Haven, 1936.

——— . "The Seneca Society of Faces." *Scientific Monthly* 44 (1937): 215–38.

——— . "Masked Medicine Societies of the Iroquois." *Annual Report of the Smithsonian Institution,* 1940, 397–430.

——— . *Songs from the Iroquois Longhouse: Program Notes for an Album of American Indian Music from the Eastern Woodlands.* Publication 3691. Washington: Smithsonian Institution, September 11, 1942.

——— . *American Indian and White Relations to 1830: Needs and Opportunities for Study.* Chapel Hill: University of North Carolina Press, 1957.

——— , ed. "Seneca Indians by Asher Wright (1859)." *Ethnohistory* 4 (Summer, 1957): 302–20.

———. *The False Faces of the Iroquois*. Norman: University of Oklahoma Press, 1987.

Fiedler, Leslie A. *The Return of the Vanishing American*. New York: Stein and Day, 1968.

Fisher, Philip. *Hard Facts: Setting and Form in the American Novel*. New York: Oxford University Press, 1987.

Fliegelman, Jay. *Prodigals and Pilgrims: The American Revolution against Patriarchal Authority, 1750–1800*. Cambridge, England: Cambridge University Press, 1982.

Foreman, Carolyn Thomas. *Indians Abroad, 1493–1938*. Norman: University of Oklahoma Press, 1943.

Foster, Michael K., et al., eds. *Extending the Rafters: Interdisciplinary Approaches to Iroquoian Studies*. Albany: State University of New York Press, 1984.

Furst, Peter T., and Jill L. Furst. *North American Indian Art*. New York: Rizzoli, 1982.

Gherman, Dawn Lander. "From Parlour to Tepee: The White Squaw on the American Frontier." Ph.D. diss., University of Massachusetts, 1975.

Gilbert, Sandra M., and Susan Gubar. *The Madwoman in the Attic: The Woman Writer and the Nineteenth-Century Literary Imagination*. New Haven: Yale University Press, 1979.

Glasrud, Bruce A., and Alan M. Smith, eds. *Race Relations in British North America, 1607–1783*. Chicago: Nelson-Hall 1982.

Graff, Harvey J., ed. *Literacy and Social Development in the West: A Reader*. Cambridge, England: Cambridge University Press, 1981.

Graymont, Barbara. *The Iroquois in the American Revolution*. Syracuse, N.Y.: Syracuse University Press, 1972.

Green, Rayna. "The Only Good Indian: The Image of the Indian in American Vernacular Culture." Ph.D. diss., Indiana University, 1973.

———. "The Pocahontas Perplex: The Image of Indian Women in American Culture." *Massachusetts Review* 16 (1975): 698–714.

———. *Native American Women: A Contextual Bibliography*. Bloomington: University of Indiana Press, 1983.

———, ed. *That's What She Said: Contemporary Poetry and Fiction by Native American Women*. Bloomington: Indiana University Press, 1984.

Grinde, Donald A., Jr. *The Iroquois and the Founding of the American Nation*. San Francisco: Indian Historian Press, 1977.

Haberly, David T. "Women and Indians: The Last of the Mohicans and the Captivity Tradition." *American Quarterly* 28 (1976): 431–43.

Hagan, William T. *American Indians.* Rev. ed. Chicago: University of Chicago Press, 1979.

Hagedorn, Nancy L. " 'A Friend to Go Between Them': The Interpreter as Cultural Broker during the Anglo-Iroquois Councils, 1740–70." *Ethnohistory* 35 (Winter, 1988): 60–80.

Halttunen, Karen. *Confidence Men and Painted Women: A Study in Middle-Class Culture in America, 1830–1870.* New Haven: Yale University Press, 1982.

Hawke, David. *The Colonial Experience.* Indianapolis: Bobbs-Merrill, 1966.

Heard, J. Norman. *White into Red: A Study of the Assimilation of White Persons Captured by Indians.* Metuchen, N.J.: Scarecrow Press, 1973.

Heilbroner, Robert L., and Aaron Singer. *The Economic Transformation of America: 1600 to the Present.* San Diego: Harcourt Brace Jovanovich, 1984.

Henretta, James A. *The Evolution of American Society, 1700–1815: An Interdisciplinary Analysis.* Lexington, Mass.: D. C. Heath, 1973.

Hernton, Calvin C. *Sex and Racism in America.* New York: Grove Press, 1965.

Herzog, Kristin. *Women, Ethnics, and Exotics: Images of Power in Mid-Nineteenth-Century American Fiction.* Knoxville: University of Tennessee Press, 1983.

Higham, John. "The Statue of Liberty, Artifact and Symbol." Comment, Seventy-ninth Annual Meeting, Organization of American Historians, New York City, April 11, 1986.

Hirsch, Adam J. "The Collision of Military Cultures in Seventeenth-Century New England." *Journal of American History* 74 (March, 1988): 1187–1212.

Honour, Hugh. *The New Golden Land: European Images of America from the Discoveries to the Present Time.* New York: Pantheon, 1975.

Horsman, Reginald. *Race and Manifest Destiny: The Origins of American Racial Anglo-Saxonism.* Cambridge, Mass.: Harvard University Press, 1981.

Hoxie, Frederick E. *Indians in American History: An Introduction.* Arlington Heights, Ill.: Harlan Davidson, 1988.

Hulton, Paul. *America, 1585: The Complete Drawings of John White.* Chapel Hill: University of North Carolina Press, 1984.

Hundley, Norris. *The American Indian: Essays from Pacific Historical Review.* Santa Barbara, Calif.: Clio Press, 1974.

Hunt, George T. *The Wars of the Iroquois: A Study in Intertribal Trade Relations.* Madison: University of Wisconsin Press, 1960, 1972.

Jaenen, Cornelius J. *Friend and Foe: Aspects of French-Amerindian Cultural Conflict in the Sixteenth and Seventeenth Centuries.* New York: Columbia University Press, 1976.

James, Edward T., Janet Wilson James, and Paul S. Boyer, eds. *Notable American Women, 1607–1950.* 2 vols. Cambridge, Mass.: Harvard University Press, 1971.

Jeffrey, Julie Roy. *Frontier Women: The Trans-Mississippi West, 1840–1880.* New York: Hill and Wang, 1979.

Jellison, Richard M. *Society, Freedom, and Conscience: The American Revolution in Virginia, Massachusetts, and New York.* New York: W. W. Norton, 1976.

Jennings, Francis. *The Invasion of America: Indians, Colonialism and the Cant of Conquest.* New York: W. W. Norton, 1976.

———. *The Ambiguous Iroquois Empire: The Covenant Chain Confederation of Indian Tribes with English Colonies from Its Beginnings to the Lancaster Treaty of 1744.* New York: W. W. Norton, 1984.

———. *Empire of Fortune: Crowns, Colonies, and Tribes in the Seven Years War in America.* New York: W. W. Norton, 1988.

Jensen, Joan M. "Native American Women in Agriculture: A Seneca Case Study." *Sex Roles* 3, no. 5 (1977): 423–41.

Johnson, Paul E. *A Shopkeeper's Millennium: Society and Revivals in Rochester, New York, 1815–1837.* New York: Hill and Wang, 1978.

Jonas, Dorothy V. *License for Empire: Colonialism by Treaty in Early America.* Chicago: University of Chicago Press, 1982.

Jones, Manfred, and Robert V. Wells, eds. *New Opportunities in a New Nation: The Development of New York after the Revolution.* Schenectady, N.Y.: Union College Press, 1982.

Kammen, Michael. *A Season of Youth: The American Revolution and the Historical Imagination.* New York: Alfred A. Knopf, 1978.

Kelsay, Isabel Thompson. *Joseph Brant, 1743–1807: Man of Two Worlds.* Syracuse, N.Y.: Syracuse University Press, 1984.

Kerber, Linda K. *Women of the Republic: Intellect and Ideology in Revolutionary America.* Chapel Hill: University of North Carolina Press, 1980.

Kerber, Linda K., and Jane De Hart Mathews, eds. *Women's America: Refocusing the Past.* 2d ed. New York: Oxford University Press, 1982.

Kinsman, Clare D. "Lois Lenski." In *Contemporary Authors: A Bio-Bibliographical Guide to Current Authors,* vol. 1. Detroit: Gale Research, 1975.

Knowles, Nathaniel. "The Torture of Captives by the Indians of Eastern North America." *Proceedings of the American Philosophical Society* 82, no. 2 (1940): 151–225.

Kolodny, Annette. *The Land before Her: Fantasy and Experience of the American Frontiers, 1630–1860.* Chapel Hill: University of North Carolina Press, 1984.

Kraft, Herbert C., ed. *A Delaware Indian Symposium.* Harrisburg: Pennsylvania Historical and Museum Collection, 1974.

Kupperman, Karen Ordahl. *Settling with the Indians: The Meeting of English and Indian Cultures in America, 1580–1640.* Totowa, N.J.: Rowman and Littlefield, 1980.

Kurath, Gertrude Prokisch. "Dance and Song Rituals of the Six Nations Reserve, Ontario." Bulletin 220, Folklore Series 4. Ottawa: National Museum of Canada, 1968.

Lauber, Almon Wheeler. *Indian Slavery in Colonial Times within the Present Limits of the United States.* New York: Columbia University, 1913.

Leach, Douglas Edward. *Flintlock and Tomahawk: New England in King Philip's War.* New York: Macmillan Company, 1958.

Leacock, Eleanor Burke. *Myths of Male Dominance: Collected Articles on Women Cross-Culturally.* New York: Monthly Review Press, 1981.

Leacock, Eleanor Burke, and Nancy Oestreich Lurie, eds. *North American Indians in Historical Perspective.* New York: Random House, 1971.

Lee, L. L., and Merrill Lewis, eds. *Women, Women Writers, and the West.* Troy, N.Y.: Whitston Publishing Co., 1979.

Lee, Susan Previant, and Peter Passell. *A New Economic View of American History.* New York: W. W. Norton, 1979.

Lerner, Gerda. *The Majority Finds Its Past: Placing Women in History.* New York: Oxford University Press, 1979.

Lismer, Marjorie. "Seneca Splint Basketry." Education Division, U.S. Office of Indian Affairs. Edited by William W. Beatty. Chilocco, Okla.: Printing Department, Chilocco Agricultural School, 1941.

Lurie, Nancy Oestreich. "Indian Cultural Adjustment to European Civilization." In James Kirby Martin, ed., *Interpreting Colonial America: Selected Readings,* 36–50. New York: Harper and Row, 1973.

Lyford, Carrie. *Iroquois Crafts.* Stevens Point, Wis.: R. Schneider, 1982.

Martin, Calvin, ed. "The Metaphysics of Writing Indian-White History." *Ethnohistory* 26 (Spring, 1979): 153–59.

————. *Keepers of the Game: Indian-Animal Relationships and the Fur Trade.* Berkeley: University of California Press, 1978.

————. *The American Indian and the Problem of History.* New York: Oxford University Press, 1987.

Mathews, Zena Pearlstone, and Aldona Jonaitis, eds. *Native North American Art History: Selected Readings.* Palo Alto, Calif.: Peek Publications, 1982.

Meade, James G. " 'The Westerns of the East': Narratives of Indian Captivity from Jeremiad to Gothic Novel." Ph.D. diss., Northwestern University, 1971.

Merrell, H. James. "The Indians' New World: The Catawba Experience" *William and Mary Quarterly* 3d ser., 41 (October, 1984): 537–65.

——— " 'The Customs of Our Countrey': Indians and Colonists in Early America." Unpublished paper.

Miller, Chris L., and George R. Hemmel. "A New Perspective on Indian-White Contact: Cultural Symbols and Colonial Trade." *Journal of American History* 73 (September, 1986): 311–28.

Miller, Nancy K. *The Heroine's Text: Readings in the French and English Novel, 1722–1782.* New York: Columbia University Press, 1980.

Minter, David L. "By Dens of Lions: Notes on Stylization in Early Puritan Captivity Narratives." *American Literature* 45 (November, 1973): 335–47.

Monaghan, E. Jennifer. "Literacy Instruction and Gender in Colonial New England." *American Quarterly* 40 (March, 1988): 18–41.

Monkman, Leslie. *A Native Heritage: Images of the Indian in English-Canadian Literature.* Toronto: University of Toronto Press, 1981.

Mott, Frank Luther. *Golden Multitudes: The Story of Best Sellers in the United States.* New York: Macmillan Company, 1947.

Namias, June. *First Generation: In the Words of Twentieth-Century American Immigrants.* Boston: Beacon Press, 1978.

——— . "Thrills, Terror, and Suffering: Responses of Captive Women, 1682–1870." Paper presented at the Sixth Berkshire Conference, Smith College, Northampton, Mass., June 3, 1984.

——— . "White Captives: Gender and Ethnicity on Successive American Frontiers, 1607–1862." Ph.D. diss. Brandeis University, 1988.

——— . *White Captives: Gender and Ethnicity on Successive American Frontiers.* Chapel Hill: University of North Carolina Press, forthcoming.

Nash, Gary B. *Red, White, and Black: The Peoples of Early America.* Englewood Cliffs, N.J.: Prentice-Hall, 1974.

——— . *The Urban Crucible: Social Change, Political Consciousness, and the Origins of the American Revolution.* Cambridge, Mass.: Harvard University Press, 1979.

Nash, Gary B., and Richard Weiss, eds. *The Great Fear: Race in the Mind of America*. New York: Holt, Rinehart and Winston, 1970.

Newberry Library. *Dictionary Catalogue of the Edward E. Ayer Collection of Americana and American Indians in the Newberry Library. And First Supplement*. Boston: G. K. Hall, 1961, 1970.

——. *The Impact of Indian History on the Teaching of United States History*. Occasional Papers in the Curriculum Series, no. 4; Washington Conference, 1985. Washington D.C.: Newberry Library, 1986.

Norton, Mary Beth. *Liberty's Daughters: The Revolutionary Experience of American Women, 1750–1800*. Boston: Little, Brown, and Company, 1980.

Parker, Arthur C. "An Analytical History of the Seneca Indians." *Researches and Transactions of the New York State Archaeological Association* 6, no. 1 (1926).

——. *The Indian How Book*. 1927. Reprint. New York: Dover, 1975.

Parry, Ellwood. *The Image of the Indian and the Black Man in American Art, 1590–1900*. New York: G. Braziller, 1974.

Paz, Octavio. *Labyrinth of Solitude: Life and Thought in Mexico*. Translated by Lysander Kemp. New York: Grove Press, 1961.

Pearce, Roy Harvey. "The Significances of the Captivity Narrative." *American Literature* 19 (March, 1947): 1–20.

——. "From the History of Ideas to Ethnohistory." *Journal of Ethnic Studies* 2 (1974): 86–92.

——. *Savagism and Civilization: A Study of the Indian and the American Mind*. Rev. ed. Berkeley: University of California Press, 1988.

Perdue, Theda. *Slavery and the Evolution of Cherokee Society, 1540–1866*. Knoxville: University of Tennessee Press, 1979.

——. "Amerindian Women: Old World Perceptions, New World Realities." Paper presented at Harvard University, March 8, 1988.

——. "Cherokee Women: A Study in Changing Gender Roles." Paper presented at the Annual Meeting of the American Historical Association, December 29, 1989.

Person, Leland S., Jr. "The American Eve: Miscegenation and a Feminist Frontier Fiction." *American Quarterly* 37 (Winter, 1985): 668–85.

Porter, H. C. *The Inconstant Savage: England and the North American Indians 1500–1660*. London: Duckworth, 1979.

Prucha, Francis Paul. *Indian-White Relations in the United States:*

A Bibliography of Works Published 1975–1980. Lincoln: University of Nebraska Press, 1982.

———. *The Great Father: The United States Government and the American Indians*. Lincoln: University of Nebraska Press, 1984.

Quain, Buell H. "The Iroquois." In Margaret Mead, ed., *Cooperation and Competition among Primitive Peoples*, 253–54. New York: McGraw-Hill, 1937.

Quinn, David Beers. *England and the Discovery of America, 1481–1620*. New York: Alfred A. Knopf, 1974.

———. *Set Fair for Roanoke: Voyages and Colonies, 1584–1606*. Chapel Hill: University of North Carolina Press, 1985.

Radway, Janice A. *Reading the Romance: Women, Patriarchy, and Popular Literature*. Chapel Hill: University of North Carolina Press, 1984.

Randle, Martha C. "Iroquois Women, Then and Now." *Bulletin of the Bureau of American Ethnology* 149 (1951): 167–80.

Ranta, Taimi M. "Lois Lenski." In *American Writers for Children, 1900–1960*, vol. 22 of the *Dictionary of Literary Biography*, edited by John Cech, 241–52. Detroit: Gale Research, 1985.

Reeve, J. C. "Henry Bouquet, His Indian Campaigns." *Ohio Archaeological and Historical Quarterly* 26 (October, 1917): 489–505.

Reiter, Rayna R., ed. *Toward an Anthropology of Women*. New York: Monthly Review Press, 1975.

Richards, Cara B. "Matriarchy or Mistake: The Role of Iroquois Women through Time." In *Cultural Stability and Cultural Change*, edited by Verne F. Ray, 36–45; Proceedings of the 1957 Annual Spring Meeting of the American Ethnological Society. Seattle: American Ethnological Society and University of Washington, 1957.

Richter, Daniel K. "War and Culture: The Iroquois Experience." *William and Mary Quarterly*, 3d ser., 40 (October, 1983): 528–59.

———. "Iroquois versus Iroquois: Jesuit Missions and Christianity in Village Politics, 1642–1686." *Ethnohistory* 32, no. 1 (1985): 1–16.

———. "Up the Cultural Stream: Three Recent Works in Iroquois Studies." *Ethnohistory* 32, no. 4 (1985): 363–69.

———. "Cultural Brokers and Intercultural Politics: New York-Iroquois Relations, 1664–1701." *Journal of American History* 75 (June, 1988): 40–67.

Richter, Daniel K., and James H. Merrell, eds. *Beyond the Covenant Chain: The Iroquois and Their Neighbors in Indian North America, 1600–1800*. Syracuse, N.Y.: Syracuse University Press, 1987.

Riley, Glenda. *Women and Indians on the Frontier, 1825–1915*. Albuquerque: University of New Mexico Press, 1984.

――――, ed. *Women in the West*. Manhattan: University of Kansas Press, 1982.

Rister, Carl Coke. *Border Captives: The Traffic in Prisoners by Southwestern Plains Indians, 1835–1875*. Norman: University of Oklahoma Press, 1940.

Rogers, Katherine. *Feminism in Eighteenth-Century England*. Urbana: University of Illinois Press, 1982.

Rogin, Michael Paul. *Fathers and Children: Andrew Jackson and the American Indian*. New York: Alfred A. Knopf, 1975.

Rohrbough, Malcolm J. *The Trans-Appalachian Frontier: People, Societies, and Institutions*. New York: Oxford University Press, 1978.

Rose, Richard. "The Morgan Collection at the Rochester Museum and Science Center." *American Indian Art* 12 (Summer, 1987): 32–37.

Rothenberg, Diane. "Erosion of Power: An Economic Basis for the Selective Conservatism of Seneca Women in the Nineteenth Century." *Western Canadian Journal of Anthropology* 6 (1976): 107–22.

Rusk, Ralph L. *The Literature of the Middle Western Frontier*. 2 vols. New York: Columbia University Press, 1925.

Ryan, Mary P. *Cradle of the Middle Class: The Family in Oneida County, New York, 1790–1865*. Cambridge, England: Cambridge University Press, 1981.

Salisbury, Neal. *Manitou and Providence: Indians, Europeans, and the Making of New England, 1500–1643*. New York: Oxford University Press, 1982.

Scott, Joan Wallach. *Gender and the Politics of History*. New York: Columbia University Press, 1988.

Segal, Charles M., and David C. Stineback. *Puritans, Indians, and Manifest Destiny*. New York: G. P. Putnam's Sons, 1977.

Shaw, Peter. *American Patriots and the Rituals of Revolution*. Cambridge, Mass.: Harvard University Press, 1981.

Sheehan, Bernard W. "Indian-White Relations in Early America: A Review Essay." *William and Mary Quarterly*, 3d ser. (1969): 267–86.

――――. *Seeds of Extinction: Jeffersonian Philanthropy and the American Indian*. Chapel Hill: University of North Carolina Press, 1973.

――――. *Savagism and Civility: Indians and Englishmen in Colonial America*. Cambridge, England: Cambridge University Press, 1980.

Shortridge, Wilson Porter. *The Transition of a Typical Frontier.*
Menasha, Wis.: George Banta Publishing, 1922.
Showalter, Elaine, ed. *The New Feminist Criticism: Essays on
Women, Literature, and Theory.* New York: Pantheon, 1985.
Silsby, Robert. *The Holland Land Company in Western New York.*
Adventures in New York History Series, no. 8. Buffalo, N.Y.:
Buffalo and Erie County Historical Society, 1961.
Slotkin, Richard. *Regeneration through Violence: The Mythology of the
American Frontier, 1600–1860.* Middletown, Conn.: Wesleyan
University Press, 1973.
————. *The Fatal Environment: The Myth of the Frontier in the Age
of Industrialization, 1800–1890.* New York: Atheneum, 1985.
Smith, Henry Nash. *Virgin Land: The American West as Symbol
and Myth.* 1950. Cambridge, Mass.: Harvard University Press,
1982.
Smith, Jane F., and Robert M. Kvasnicka, eds. *Indian-White Rela-
tions: A Persistent Paradox.* Washington, D.C.: Howard Univer-
sity Press, 1981.
Smith, Robinson V. "New Hampshire Persons Taken as Captives
by the Indians." *Historical New Hampshire* 8 (March, 1952): 24–
36.
Smith, Sidonie. *A Poetics of Women's Autobiography: Marginality
and the Fictions of Self-Representation.* Bloomington: Indiana
University Press, 1987.
Smith-Rosenberg, Carroll. *Disorderly Conduct: Visions of Gender in
Victorian America.* New York: Alfred A. Knopf, 1985.
Snyderman, George S. *Behind the Tree of Peace: A Sociological Analy-
sis of Iroquois Warfare.* Ph.D. diss., University of Pennsylvania.
1948. Reprint. New York: AMS Press, 1979.
Sollors, Werner. *Beyond Ethnicity: Consent and Descent in American
Culture.* New York: Oxford University Press, 1986.
Speck, Frank Gouldsmith. *Oklahoma Delaware Ceremonies, Feasts,
and Dances.* Memoirs of the American Philosophical Society, vol.
7. Philadelphia: American Philosophical Society, 1937.
————. *The Iroquois: A Study in Cultural Evolution.* Cranbrook
Institute of Science Bulletin 23. Bloomfield Hills, Mich., Octo-
ber, 1945.
Starna, William A., and Ralph Watkins. "Northern Iroquoian Slav-
ery." *Ethnohistory* 38 (Winter, 1991): 34–57.
Stedman, Raymond William. *Shadows of the Indian: Stereotypes
in American Culture.* Norman: University of Oklahoma Press,
1982.
Stocking, George W. *Victorian Anthropology.* New York: Free
Press, 1987.

Strecker, Fredrick. *My First Years as a Jemisonian.* Rochester, N.Y.: Fredrick Strecker, 1931.

Strong, Pauline Turner. "Captive Images: Stereotypes that Justified Colonial Expansion on the American Frontier Were a Legacy of a Seventeenth-Century War." *Natural History,* December, 1985, 51–56.

————. "Captivated by the Other: English Representations of Identity and Power in Colonial North America, 1682–1736." Paper presented to the Western Social Science Association, Denver, April 28, 1988.

Sturtevant, William C., ed. *Handbook of North American Indian Indians.* 15 vols. Washington D.C.: Smithsonian Institution, 1978–.

Suleiman, Susan R., and Inge Crosman, eds. *The Reader in the Text: Essays on Audience and Interpretation.* Princeton: Princeton University Press, 1980.

Swagerty, W. R., ed. *Scholars and the Indian Experience: Critical Reviews of Recent Writing in the Social Sciences.* Bloomington: University of Indiana Press, 1984.

Tanner, Helen Hornbeck. "Coocoochee: Mohawk Medicine Woman." *American Indian Culture and Research Journal* 3, no. 3 (1979): 23–41.

Tebbel, John. *The Creation of an Industry, 1630–1865.* Vol. I, *A History of Book Publishing in the United States.* New York: R. R. Bowker-Xerox, 1972.

Thernstrom, Stephan, ed. *Harvard Encyclopedia of American Ethnic Groups.* 2 vols. Cambridge, Mass.: Harvard University Press, 1980.

Thomas, G. E. "Puritans, Indians, and the Concept of Race." *New England Quarterly* 48 (March, 1975): 3–27.

Thornton, Russell. "American Indian Historical Demography: A Review Essay with Suggestions for Further Research." *American Indian Culture and Research Journal* 3, no. 1 (1976): 69–74.

Tocqueville, Alexis de. *Democracy in America.* Henry Reeve text, translated by Phillips Bradley. 2 vols. New York: Vintage-Random House, 1961.

Todorov, Tzvetan. *The Conquest of America: The Question of the Other.* Translated by Richard Howard. New York: Harper and Row, 1982.

Tompkins, Jane P. *Sensational Designs: The Cultural Work of American Fiction, 1790–1860.* New York: Oxford University Press, 1985.

Tooker, Elisabeth, ed. "The Iroquois White Dog Sacrifice in the Latter Part of the Eighteenth Century." *Ethnohistory* 11 (Spring 1965): 129–40.

———— . *The Iroquois in the American Revolution: 1976 Conference Proceedings*. Research Records, no. 14. Rochester, N.Y.: Rochester Museum and Science Center, 1981.

Trelease, Allen W. *Indian Affairs in Colonial New York: The Seventeenth Century*. Ithaca, N. Y.: Cornell University Press, 1960.

———— . "Mary Jemison." *Notable American Women, 1607–1950*, 2:271–73. Edited by Edward T. James et al. Cambridge, Mass.: Harvard University Press, 1971.

Trigger, Bruce G. *The Children of Aataentsic: A History of the Huron People to 1660*. 2 vols. Montreal: McGill-Queen's University Press, 1976.

———— , ed. *Northeast*. Vol. 15, *Handbook of North American Indians*, edited by William C. Sturtevant. Washington D.C.: Smithsonian Institution, 1978.

Ulrich, Laurel Thatcher. *Good Wives: Image and Reality in the Lives of Women in Northern New England, 1650–1750*. New York: Alfred A. Knopf, 1982.

Underhill, Ruth M. *Red Man's America: A History of Indians in the United States*. Rev. ed. Chicago: University of Chicago Press, 1971.

Vail, R. W. G. "Certain Indian Captives of New England." *Massachusetts Historical Society Proceedings* 68 (1944–47): 113–31.

VanDerBeets, Richard. "The Indian Captivity Narrative: An American Genre." Ph.D. diss., University of the Pacific, 1973.

———— . *The Indian Captivity Narrative: An American Genre*. Lanham, Md.: University Press of America, 1984.

Vanderhoof, E. W. *Historical Sketches of Western New York*. Buffalo, N.Y.: Matthews-Northrup Works, 1907.

Van Kirk, Sylvia. *Many Tender Ties: Women in Fur Trade Society, 1670–1870*. 1980. Norman: University of Oklahoma Press, 1989.

Vaughan, Alden T. *New England Frontier: Puritans and Indians, 1620–1675*. Rev. ed. New York: W. W. Norton, 1979.

———— . "From White Man to Redskin: Changing Anglo-American Perceptions of the American Indian." *American Historical Review* 87 (October, 1982): 917–53.

Vaughan, Alden T., with Oscar Handlin, ed. *American Genesis: Captain John Smith and the Founding of Virginia*. Boston: Little, Brown and Company, 1975.

Vaughan, Alden T., and Daniel K. Richter. "Crossing the Cultural Divide: Indians and New Englanders, 1605–1763." *Proceedings of the American Antiquarian Society* 90 (April 16, 1980): 23–99.

Vecsey, Christopher. *Imagine Ourselves Richly: Mythic Narratives of North American Indians*. New York: Crossroad, 1988.

Vecsey, Christopher, and Robert W. Venables, eds. *American In-*

dian Environments: Ecological Issues in Native American History. Syracuse, N.Y.: Syracuse University Press, 1980.

Verlinden, Charles. *The Beginnings of Modern Civilization: Eleven Essays with an Introduction*. Translated by Yvonne Freccero. Ithaca, N. Y.: Cornell University Press, 1970.

Vicinus, Martha. "Heroines for 19th Century Girls: Popular Biographies of Florence Nightingale." Paper presented at the Seventh Berkshire Conference, Wellesley College, Wellesley, Mass., June 20, 1987.

Wallace, Anthony F. C. *The Death and Rebirth of the Seneca*. 1969. New York: Random-Vintage, 1972.

Warner, Michael. "Literary Studies and the History of the Book." *The Book: Newsletter of the Program in History of the Book in American Culture Published by the American Antiquarian Society* 12 (July, 1987): 3–9.

Washburn, Wilcomb. E. *Red Man's Land/White Man's Law: A Study of the Past and Present Status of the American Indian*. New York: Charles Scribner's Sons, 1971.

———. *The Indian in America*. New York: Harper and Row, 1975.

Washburn, Wilcomb E., ed. *History of Indian-White Relations*. Vol. 4, *Handbook of North American Indians*, edited by William C. Sturtevant. Washington, D.C.: Smithsonian Institution, 1988.

Waugh, Fredrick W. *Iroquois Foods and Food Preparation*. Canada Department of Mines, Anthropological Series, no. 12. 1916. Reprint. Ottawa: National Museum of Canada, 1973.

Weslager, C. A. *The Log Cabin in America: From Pioneer Days to the Present*. New Brunswick, N.J.: Rutgers University Press, 1969.

White, Lonnie J. "White Women Captives of Southern Plains Indians, 1866–1875." *Journal of the West* 8, no. 3 (July, 1969): 327–54.

Wilson, Eva. *North American Indian Designs*. London: British Museum Publications, 1984.

Wolf, Eric R. *Europe and the People Without History*. Berkeley: University of California Press, 1982.

Young, Alfred F., ed. *The American Revolution: Explorations in the History of American Radicalism*. De Kalb: Northern Illinois University Press, 1976.

Young, Mary E. "Women, Civilization, and the Indian Question." In *Women's America: Refocusing the Past*, edited by Linda K. Kerber and Jane De Hart Mathews, 149–55. New York: Oxford University Press, 1982.

Zeisberger, David. *History of the North American Indians*. Edited by Archer Butler Herbert and William N. Schwartze. Columbus, Ohio: Fred J. Herr, 1910.

Index

Abenaki Indians, 7
Adams, John, 23
African Americans: 105–106
Agriculture: beans in, 22, 80; corn in, 22, 28–29, 79, 80, 81, 84; cows in, 91, 159; grain in, 122; squash in, 22, 80; women's responsibility for, 17–22, 79–80, 81, 83–84, 85, 97, 105, 141–42, 159
Albany, N.Y., 145
Alcohol, effect of, on Indians, 31–33, 84–85, 114, 124–27, 140–41, 148, 158–59
Allegany, N.Y., 147
Allegheny River, 25, 73
Allen, Ebenezer, 149; captured, 114; crimes of, 117–18; on De Trench River, 116–17; to Gardow Tract, 109–10, 112; to Mount Morris, 112, 114–16; Nettle's attempts to capture, 111–14; in Seven Years' War, 110–11; wives of, 115–16
Allen, Lucy: 115–17
Allen, Sally, 112, 115–17
Allen's Creek, 115, 116
American Civil War, 4, 34
American Revolution, 17, 53, 55, 96, 117, 159; captive-taking in, 99–100, 103–104; Iroquois disunity during, 23, 27; Senecas during, 23, 27–30, 106–108. See also Seven Years' War
Antler, Joyce, 13
Auburn, N.Y., 4
Axtell, James, 18
Aztec Indians, 8

Banister, Daniel, 55
Batavia, N.Y., 4
Berry, Jack, 108
Big Kettle (Sun-ge-waw): 150
Big Lance. See Hiokatoo
Big Tree, 33; Council at, 95, 120; treaty of, 31, 117
Black Chief, 149
Black Coals. See Kaujisestaugeau
Boone, Daniel and Jemima, 7
Boone, Hawkins, 131
Boyd, William, 103

185

ACL-3941